DROPS
from a
LEAKING
TAP

DROPS
from a
LEAKING
TAP

GEORGE VERWER

Authentic

HYDERABAD · COLORADO SPRINGS · LONDON

Drops from a Leaking Tap
by George Verwer

Copyright © 2008 by George Verwer

First Indian edition 2008
ISBN: 978-81-7362-844-3

Published by Authentic Books

P. O. Box 2190, Secunderabad 500 003, Andhra Pradesh.
www.authenticindia.in

9 Holdom Avenue, Bletchley, Milton Keynes, MK1 1QR, UK
www.authenticmedia.co.uk

1820 Jet Stream Drive, Colorado Springs, CO 80921, USA.
www.authenticbooks.com

Scripture references are taken from The Holy Bible, *King James Version.* Some of the Scripture references are taken from The Holy Bible, *Revised Standard Version.* Yet other Scripture references are taken from the *New International Version* (NIV). Copyright © 1973, 1978, 1984 by International Bible Society.

Authentic Books is an imprint of Authentic India, the publishing division of IBS-STL OM Books India.

Contents

Foreword

This wonderful collection of messages is vintage George Verwer. I am delighted that Authentic Media are releasing this collection because it contains chapters that faithfully capture both the old and the new emphases of George's ministry.

George Verwer's evolution as a missionary statesman and a man of God has been a great encouragement to me. George has always remained a learner and this has been a model for all of us who have been impacted by his leadership. The content of this book reveals what George has learned over 50 years of ministry.

Even though George is 70 years old he continues as ever, taking the message God has given him to the church worldwide. While many of us in India now have the opportunity to hear George in person, this book gives many people the opportunity to be exposed to the revolutionary message God gave this man.

For those of you interested in OM's history you will find snippets all over the place in this collection. Enjoy the story. A full length book on OM's history has just been released in the West and is now available in India from Authentic Media.

I trust this book will be a blessing to you.

Dr. Joseph D'souza,
President, OM India Group of Ministries.

Introduction

As I type this I am about to turn 70 years of age. My birthday, July 3, is the same day and same year as Alfy Franks who led the work in India for many years and has continued with his wife Addy to be two of our most faithful coworkers and friends. This book which we have been working on for some years is written specifically for India. Due to my own stupidity (there was no sin involved) and my unwillingness to pay a bribe to Bombay customs, my name ended up on the *persona non grata* list and this has kept me all these years from visiting my beloved India. Meanwhile hundreds of thousands of copies of my books, *Literature Evangelism, There's Dynamite in Literature, Revolution of Love, Hunger for Reality, No Turning Back* and *Out of the Comfort Zone* have gone out in many languages all over the country. The letters and now emails have poured in from all over India and I have tried to answer all of them, mixing it with prayer.

Do not expect this book to flow like most books. It is more of a compendium of articles mainly by myself, but also from a few other people whom I really want to thank. I have actually written more for this book than any other except *Literature Evangelism.* My other books were all largely taken from my tapes and then reworked by myself and an editor. You might want to go to the index and just read a chapter that seems to grab you. If you tick it off after you read it. . .and read, say a chapter a day or even a week or month, then some day you may finish it all, but don't worry if you don't. The chapter on "Pain" or "7 Global Scourges" for me is worth all the effort we have put into the book. You can also copy anything you want and pass it on, with permission from Authentic Media.

My second book, *Hunger for Reality,* over these 40 years has brought me over 25,000 letters and I read and answered most of them. They still come and what I have said in my books is still relevant and important today. All these 53 years in Christ I have tried to live out an hour by hour basis that which I have tried to share in this book. I really hope and pray it will be a blessing to you and your friends. I mention other books and I hope you will read many of them. I hope you will also spend some time visiting my web site: www.georgeverwer.com

Thanks.

In his grace and grip,

George Verwer.

Chapter 1

———❖———

Continuing the Revolution of Love
(Interview with Dan Wooding, 2003)

George Verwer, the colorful New Jersey-native and Founder and International Coordinator of Operation Mobilisation (OM), a worldwide ministry of evangelism, discipleship training and church planting, has just become a British Old Aged Pensioner and is also about to handover the leadership of OM.

Verwer, who celebrated his 65th birthday on July 3, "passed the mantle" onto British-born Peter Maiden, who became the International Director of OM in the Keswick Convention tent in the British Lake District, where some 2,000 OM leaders and supporters attended.

"Peter Maiden has proven a strong leader in God for over twenty years as he originally led the work in the UK," Verwer said in a trans-Atlantic phone interview. "It is with great peace and joy that I pass on my leadership responsibilities on to him."

Verwer went on to say that although he is handing over the leadership of OM and will be picking up a small UK old age pension, he is not retiring from ministry.

Leader to the "Whole Body of Christ"

"There is no retirement involved as a main chunk of my work is already writing, teaching, preaching and fund raising, and all those things will continue. But I will not be leading OM from the closet," said Verwer. "I will not be the chairman of the board. I really have full peace in my heart to pull back from all OM leadership. I hope now to be a leader in the whole Body of Christ as an example. I will have more time as I am involved with many other mission agencies. I am very much involved in the World Evangelical Alliance because I am the chairman of the Mission Mobilization Network which used to be part of A.D. 2000 and now it's part of the Mission Commission of WEA.

"I will now get a few Pounds from the British Old Age Pension. My wife Drena and I have always lived on our support. For the past 15 years, we have been able to live on 20 percent of our support and give 80 percent to literature and keep the work going.

"The Movement is letting me keep a small team called Special Projects Ministries which I have been operating for 30 years. It's a benevolent networking fund through which I have financed literature and other media projects—medium sized and small; that includes a whole new thing that I am doing with HIV/AIDS. This is one of the things I really hope to give more time to in the future."

How He Found Christ

George Verwer became a believer at the age of 16 in a Jack Wyrtzen meeting in which Billy Graham spoke in Madison Square Garden, New York. He returned to his school in northern New Jersey. Within a year about 200 of his classmates had found a relationship with the living God through Jesus Christ.

George had a growing conviction to share the Word of God on foreign soil. He started with distribution of Gospel of John in

Mexico along with two friends. This continued with others during summer holidays—beginning in Mexico in 1957.

Attending Maryville College after high school, he transferred to Moody Bible Institute where he met a girl, Drena, a fellow student who later became his wife. They were led together in discipling young Christians, while concurrently carrying out a rigorous program of world evangelism.

Verwer then gave some of the highlights of the extraordinary ministry of OM:

"1957—This is one of the most important years in my life as we evangelized door to door and other ways in New Jersey. With the Billy Graham Crusade in New York City, leaving immediately for Mexico, Walter Borchard, Dale Rhoton and myself were to experience amazing answers to prayer, discovering that God could use even young people in a foreign country. We had met in a providential way at Maryville College, where I got involved in all kinds of ministry; and experienced greater reality in the Holy Spirit and the Word of God that continued to change my life.

"1958—Dale Rhoton transferred to Wheaton College in the fall of 1957 and we followed six months later, with Walter also going to Wheaton and my going to Moody Bible Institute. I was soon to meet Drena Knecht who on January 31, 1960 became my wife. She also went to Mexico the previous summer and Christmas. I met four others at Moody who went back to Mexico that summer and we started our first bookshop and other ministries especially in Monterrey and Saltillo. Baldemar Aguilar became our first full-time worker. A small group of business people back in New Jersey set up a Board and legally registered under the name I felt God gave me, Send The Light.

"1959—We took meetings around Chicago sharing the vision. Nights of prayer were born at Moody, which soon had a focus on the unreached peoples and especially the Communist world and Muslim world. Again during summer and Christmas we were back in Mexico with large groups in different cities reaching hundreds of thousands with the Word of God and opening more Christian bookshops.

"1960—The vision had spread to Wheaton, Emmaus and other colleges, and Dale Rhoton after thoughts about other directions, came into the work and made a commitment to the forgotten, needy land of Turkey. He soon was to be joined by others like Roger Malstead. Drena and I immediately after marriage headed back to Mexico with the vision of more shops and ministries and turned it all over to Mexicans and Dick and Helen Griffin who were to soon go there long term; they have been there ever since. After a summer, spreading the vision in the USA, we headed for Spain and on October 29, God gave us our son Benjamin. We soon opened an unusual bookshop as well as other ministries especially flooding the Word of God across all of Spain via the post. A small number of Spaniards joined us by faith and the work grew very quickly.

"1961—That summer was to change my life because due to a silly mistake Roger Malstead and I were arrested by the Soviet police and the KGB and accused us of being spies. After deciding we were religious people they took us to the Austrian border. During a day of prayer God gave me the vision and the name— Operation Mobilisation. We wanted to mobilize God's people in Europe to reach their own continent and then spread into the Muslim and Communist world. A dozen or so people joined from the United States and together with a few Spaniards, we had the first European conference in Madrid. We decided to go ahead by faith and drafted a Manifesto that got distributed around the world. Teams headed out to many countries, including Turkey, which became a priority field.

"1962—At the end of 1961 I took a strategic trip back to Mexico and the USA. In early 1962 Drena, Ben and I, moved to London where God quickly opened many doors. By the summer about 200 people gathered in Paris and moved out across Europe with over 25 million pieces of literature in many languages. This was the first Operation Mobilisation and the name has stuck with us ever since. In September a much bigger group gathered in Madrid and we waited on God about the future.

"1963—In some ways this was OM's turning point, which brought close to 2,000 people to the summer mobilization and evangelization. We soon had over 100 vehicles with teams and literature on the road. At the end of the summer our main conferences shifted to the north of England where a UK Board of Directors was formed. The first teams for India headed out overland from this conference, which in those days was a very difficult journey taking up to a month. I was to meet them in New Delhi in January and this proved to be a life-changing experience for me. Within a few weeks of traveling around India, I felt this was the place that God wanted Drena and me to be.

"1964—Daniel was born in November 1962 after which we moved to the Netherlands to help in the preparations for that summer campaign. Christa was born on June 30 and by September we were all in India as a family, based in Bombay. We ministered all over the nation, of course, with a team of others like Greg Livingstone and Thomas Samuel. This was the beginning of what would become OM's largest and, in some ways, most fruitful field. A major literature ministry was birthed simultaneously with all the other aspects of ministry enabling us in the years to come to give the Word of God to literally hundreds of millions of precious people.

"1965—For the next three years we were to spend half the year in India and half in Europe. More coworkers were staying for the year and longer-term programs, and each September we started the new year in OM with a leadership training and a new recruits' conference. This was to continue for a couple of decades and led eventually to over 100,000 people taking part in OM. The work in the UK was in two sections, with Keith Beckwith leading the basic OM work and John Watts leading the literature work which went under the old name of Send the Light or STL. In December 1966 they were both killed in a car accident in Poland which led us to come back to London, asking Gerry and Jean Davey to return from Spain to take up the challenge of STL.

"1966—At the September conference, in a small room in a pub in Bolton, Lancashire that we had converted into a Christian bookshop, the idea first came to us about getting an ocean-going ship. I shared it with only a small group of leaders and we knew we had to wait on the Lord and do lots of research, which went on for the next couple of years. Meanwhile, the work continued to grow in many different countries including the nations behind the Iron Curtain as Dale Rhoton had to leave Turkey and he became the director of the work in Eastern Europe.

"1967—The work in India was growing very rapidly and much of our early thinking about the ship was in connection with our burden and vision for India. I was soon to become persona non grata due to my own blunders and some false reports. But what seemed like a setback was a further push to make sure the work was built on Indian leadership. Alfy Franks and Ray Eicher stepped into the main leadership role, with me acting as the area leader for two more decades, often meeting in Nepal with the leaders who came from all over India.

"1968—Refused entry into India, we ended up living and ministering in Nepal. We operated under the name EBE (Educational Books Exhibits) which later became an official company and responsible for the first ship. Many of the summer efforts in Europe and other places had a greater emphasis on follow-up and church planting. In France especially, Mike Evans, who was surely one of our most outstanding leaders, wanted to see more churches planted. He led us in a huge effort to touch every part of France in the summers of '70 and '71. A French publishing house called Farel was born, that later became independent and continues to this day.

"1969—Jonathan McRostie was doing a great job coordinating the work in Europe and the summer campaigns continued every summer with more people wanting to stay on for a year or longer. Of course, there were always plenty of problems and often a great shortfall of finance. Sometimes under pressure there were tensions and divisions, but repeatedly we saw amazing answers to prayer and it was clear that God had bonded together a long-term staff that would enable us to do a better job with all those who were coming for short term. The work in Mexico continued under Dick Griffin, and Paul and Ilse Troper were to lead the work in the USA for about two decades. It was always clear that we had more lessons to learn, especially about grace.

"1970—Moving on progressively, some of us felt that now was the hour for the ship, and I circulated a memo to that effect with a photo of a ship. Captain Graham Scott joined us and was helping present this faith vision in different churches. Money started coming in and other crew members were signing up. In October of that year we purchased the *Umanak* from the Danish Government and it became Logos. I would urge you to read *The Logos Story*, the book about this ship and her ministry until we lost her in 1988.

"1971—Drena and I, with our family, moved to the ship Logos in Rotterdam where she was repaired and refurbished and we were soon on our way around the whole of Africa to India. This was to be one of the most stretching and exciting years of our lives. As we sailed into Cochin Harbor, the OMers came out to meet us in small boats, I began to weep with praise and thanksgiving. A new and effective ministry had been born which was to grow beyond our expectations with Doulos being added in 1977 and later Logos II in 1990 (and now Logos Hope in 2008)."

He concluded by saying, "I still believe with all my heart that evangelism is a top priority, but the biggest change that has happened in OM during the last decade is that we have accepted from the Lord that we are to be a holistic ministry. We must be concerned about the whole person of a human being. So OM is transformed and some people are worried about it. We are into earthquake and flood relief work and into helping the poor. We are also into the HIV/AIDS challenge. Every field is finding its own ministry strengths even as every field has to find its own money. We know there are problems, even though we are doing this and have received this from the Word and from other men and women who have helped us. We are a movement influenced by many godly people.

"Evangelism and prayer must be in our whole movement. Our whole movement is 100 percent committed to evangelism. It does seem that I, as an older person moving out of the leadership, that OM can still be alive and well."

Dan Wooding is an award-winning British journalist now living in Southern California with his wife Norma. He is the founder and International Director of ASSIST (Aid to Special Saints in Strategic Times). Wooding is also a syndicated columnist, and was for ten years a commentator on the UPI Radio Network in Washington, DC. Wooding is the author of some 41 books, one of which is *Blind Faith* which he coauthored with his 93-year-old mother Anne Wooding, who was a pioneer missionary to the blind of Nigeria in the 1930's. Copies of this book are available from the ASSIST USA office at PO Box 2126, Garden Grove, CA 92842-2 126. His writings are on the ASSIST Website at: www.assistnews.net

Chapter 2

Operation Mobilisation– The Beginning

Operation Mobilisation traces its roots to the prayers of an ordinary American housewife. In the 1950's, Dorothea Clapp began to pray faithfully for the students in her local high school. She asked God to touch the world through the lives of those young people, and God answered her prayers!

Mrs. Clapp specifically prayed for a student, George Verwer, that he would be saved and sent out as a missionary. She sent him a Gospel of John through mail, and he later gave his life to the Lord at a Billy Graham meeting. That young man George Verwer, became the Founder and former International Director of Operation Mobilisation.

While attending Maryville College, George and two friends met regularly to pray and they became burdened by the spiritual needs of Mexico. In 1957, the three friends sold some of their possessions to raise money and gave up their summer holidays to distribute Gospels and other Christian literature in Mexico. The next school year, George transferred to Moody Bible Institute and his two friends to Wheaton College. They returned to Mexico the following summer and the next.

When he graduated from Moody in 1960, George and his friends traveled to Europe. They began work in Spain, sharing the gospel and distributing literature, but the task of reaching the whole of Europe seemed overwhelming.

George and his small team realized that God's plan was to mobilize his church to reach the nations. As they began to share their vision, hundreds of Christians responded, and Operation Mobilisation was born.

By 1963, 2,000 Christians had joined the summer outreach teams in Europe. At the same time, the first year teams moved into the Indian sub-continent and the Muslim world. Their commitment was to reach those who had never heard the gospel.

Such simple beginnings have shaped OM ever since. Today over 5,000 OMers are working in 100 countries bringing God's unchanging truth to literally millions every year.

Chapter 3

Embracing the Pain

I have a great burden on my heart and want to share it with as many people as possible.

I am burdened for people who are hurting in a major way. We all have hurts, but there are so many who are hurting much more than the others.

Often, when we want to help or minister to such people it seems not possible because their hurts have created a barrier or wall and they can't get through it. Some Christians have been hurt so much by other Christians, that they will not go to church or fellowship with other believers. For them, it is all too painful.

There are many great books and passages of Scripture that can help such people, but they might not know about them and are hesitant to read them. The book, *Life of the Beloved* by Henri J.M. Nouwen has ministered to me in a powerful way. Henri Nouwen speaks of finding the courage to embrace our own brokenness and make our feared enemy into a friend, even claiming it as an intimate companionship.

Shortly after reading it, I had a very painful experience with a friend who deeply criticized one of my closest friends. It could have really upset me and ruined our time together, but instead, I embraced it as allowed by God and part of what life is all about. Great joy and peace flooded my heart and I was free. I know it doesn't always work that way and that others have hurts a hundred times greater than mine, yet they are not too big for God.

How can we who are forgiven of our sins and delivered from hell, not truly forgive with our whole being those who have sinned against us? We know that all sin, and we teach and preach over it. So, why are we surprised when people sin against us?

We all fail. We all sin. Can we not see our own sins that are so often part of the hurt and pain that we are now living with? Oh, how easy for the self-life to blame others and fail to see our part in the situation.

In some cases, people are blaming God and that becomes even more complex. Books like, *Disappointment with God* by Philip Yancey etc., have been written to help deal with this.

There is great hope for all of us. God has used us and he has a great plan for our lives in our pilgrimage to become more like Christ, which should always be our great goal!

Let us embrace the pain and hurt and allow them to make us better people for his glory.

Chapter 4

Big Transition

In August 2003, we had a great OM conference at Keswick with about two thousand people. After 46 years of leading OM, I had the joy of turning over the leadership to Peter Maiden.

Some people worried how I would react to this adjustment in my life. As I thought about this, seven key words came to mind. They speak of the grace, motivation, and reality I have experienced during this change in roles. They also speak of the continuance with my journey so far.

The first word is quite simply. . .

Change

I'm a great believer in change. I have been blessed to help lead many major changes we have made in the entire work of OM over the years. I learned to accept change even when I didn't initially agree. Marriage has helped me learn this! At times of change, relationships can be challenged. Unity is so important; God's unity is in the midst of great diversity. I have learned that unity has a complex price tag that sometimes involves compromise and yielding to the plans and ideas of others.

People

I have as many opportunities to love and serve people now as I did before. In fact, the reality is that now I have more freedom in whom I serve and how I go about it! It may sound strange to some, but even though I was heading up a mission organization, a lot of my efforts needed to be put into spending very necessary time with other leaders and other Christians. Now that I am released from those responsibilities I'm actually getting more time with people who do not know Christ, and that of course, is the heart of mission.

Prayer

Almost since my conversion, about 50 years ago, this has been one of my greatest passions. I now have just as much opportunity for this as ever. In fact, I'm able to find more time to pray now, which includes worship, praise as well as intercession.

Preaching

I started to preach at 17 and now more than 20,000 messages later, I still sense God's call to preach and teach. In God's mercy I am flooded with invitations from around the globe. Since my role changed I have had hundreds of meetings and hope to continue in this as long as I have the voice and strength.

Projects

OM has allowed me to continue with projects all over the world. These are mainly concerned with literature and audio visuals. I have a small field structure and the responsibility with a small team raising money for projects as well as coordinating them. I always seem to have four times more work than I can handle—but I am really happy with the challenge! There is not much time to think about my old leadership role.

Trust

I have a deep trust, which is linked with faith, that the work I have been involved with all these years is God's work and I believe he will continue to have his hand upon it.

Vision

My vision has not changed, only my role. The vision for prayer, mobilization, world evangelism, and discipleship remain extremely strong. I can honestly say that it is a motivating factor almost every hour of every day. God has added to that a greater vision and commitment to social concern and action.

That's the answer to the question of how I am doing. But this isn't all about me, we all live in times of great change. In closing, I pray that those who read this and those going through a transition or change in their own lives will lay hold of God's grace in a powerful way. I've always had many weaknesses and struggles in my Christian life and still have much to learn. I believe if a needy character like me can keep running the race in my senior years, then no one has an excuse not to! Let's keep on keeping on.

Chapter 5

Failure, the Back Door to Success

The KGB officer in charge of my interrogation said I was a spy. "We have a place for American spies," he told me. "It's called Siberia."

Things were not going well. The Soviets had our vehicle. They were interrogating my partner, Roger, in another room. It was just a matter of time before they would discover the Bibles and the printing press we had smuggled into the heart of the Communist world.

It was 1961 and the Cold War was in full swing. My dream of taking the Gospel into closed countries—not to mention my life— could come to a very quick end. What to do?

Anybody who knew me wouldn't be surprised at the predicament I was in. People called me a radical. Ever since my conversion in 1955 at a Billy Graham meeting in New York City, I was diving head first into any opportunity I could find to share the gospel. Shortly after my conversion I got a chance to speak to the entire student body of my high school, and used it to share Jesus. I shared my faith going door to door. I organized rallies—600 people came to one rally, 125 professed their faith in Christ (including my own father). In 1957 I arranged to get people to the Billy Graham meeting literally by the busload, but I myself did not attend the crusade. Since every seat was taken, I did not want to take a seat that could be occupied by a non-Christian. So, while Billy Graham preached in Madison Square Garden, I went out into the streets of New York City and preached. Then later, with two friends, I took off to evangelize Mexico.

It just made sense. Why not go to some place where people haven't heard the gospel?

In those days, Mexico was a semi-closed country. Protestants were persecuted. Importing Christian literature was illegal. Our car was loaded with literature and we had no idea how we were going to get across the border. But we got across. We prayed much, stuffed the literature under our mattresses, crossed the border at night, and they waved us through.

We worked among people living in the garbage dumps. The enormous poverty witnessed there gripped me. As I watched flies crawling across the eyes of little babies, my heart cried out to God: "What can I do to awaken this nation to the life-changing gospel of Jesus Christ?" We decided to get on the radio. There was only one problem, in Mexico Christian radio was illegal. I thought, there's got to be a way around this!

I returned to the United States, transferred from my liberal arts college to Moody Bible Institute, organized a team of five and headed back to Mexico. Before we left we prayed and when we got to Mexico, God gave us a plan. We started a bookstore and went to the local radio station saying, "We represent a bookstore and we want to advertise. We sell Bibles. The reason why people don't buy the Bible is that they don't know what's in it. We'd like to read from it in our advertisement." It worked. We read and explained the Scriptures over Mexican radio. That was the beginning of a weekly 15-minute program.

Back at Moody, I prayed, planned, organized and read missionary books. I dreamed about getting into countries like Iraq and Afghanistan. There was hardly any Christian there—it was the perfect opportunity!

I didn't want romance to derail me, so I went on what I called a "social fast" (seeking God's choice)—No dating! That lasted for two years. Then one day I met Drena a staff member at Moody. My social fast ended immediately. I was in love!

I wanted to make sure that Drena shared my radical commitment to world missions and so on our first meeting I said to her, "Probably nothing is going to happen between us, but I'm going to be a missionary, and if you marry me, you'll probably end up being eaten by cannibals in New Guinea."

She was definitely not in love with me, but I persisted. Eventually, we got engaged. I never wanted to spend any money, because I wanted even the smallest coin of money to go to the gospel. "Why buy meals when Moody provides them" was my mindset. One day when we were out together sitting by Lake Michigan (I often skipped meals, but I didn't think it was right to ask her to skip a meal), I asked the Lord if he would somehow supply food for her without us having to spend any money. The people sitting behind us were having a picnic, they packed up and left. I went to the wastebasket, pulled out the brown paper bag which they discarded, and discovered a sandwich which was not unwrapped. I gave it to my fiancée. She got a real taste of what she was getting married to!

We were married in Milwaukee in 1960[1] just after I graduated. At that time, I hardly believed in marriage ceremonies, so we had our wedding after the Sunday morning church service that the pastor could preach the gospel to the non-Christians present. During the

---

[1] I finished in two years by transferring some credits and taking some courses by correspondence. I remember sitting in the bus station, supposedly on a date with Drena, working on correspondence courses.

reception, my close friend Dale Rhoton, stood up and said, "The main thing you can give George and Drena is prayer, because they're selling everything else for the sake of the gospel."[2]

We skipped the honeymoon and headed to Mexico. On our way, we decided not to spend any money. The first night I took our wedding cake to a gas station in Wheaton, offering the cake for gas. They filled the tank and let me keep the cake. The next morning, another station owner too—a Christian—let me keep the cake. The next guy was not so generous, he liked the cake and we traded the cake for gas. We got all the way to Mexico without spending a cent.

Over the next six months we opened bookstores and evangelized. Then we moved to another closed country, Spain. Spain, under Franco, had little toleration for gospel. So we made it our home base while I studied Russian and prepared to launch into the Soviet Union.

The plan for the Soviet Union was simple. Roger Malstead and I smuggled Scripture portions and a printing press in. Then we planned to mail the Gospels to addresses taken from the phone book. Things were going well, until I accidentally spilled melted butter on one of the Gospels, rendering it unusable.

"Flush it down the toilet," Roger suggested.

But I hated wasting that Scripture. "I know what to do," I thought, "I'll find some isolated spot in the countryside where no one can see us, and I'll throw it out the window. Then someone can pick it up and read it!"

That was a big mistake. Someone did see us. Within ten miles, we were stopped at a major roadblock and arrested as spies. They interrogated us for two days. I decided to tell them the truth. When

---

[2]I have since come to see that giving away everything for the sake of the gospel can turn into a twisted and legalistic rule. Some, for example, feel it is unspiritual to maintain an attractive home, but I have found that a beautiful (though not extravagant) home can be a good witness to our neighbors of the joy we have in Jesus Christ.

they found the printing press and all our other literature hidden in our car, they freaked out.

We were the headline news in Soviet Russia. *Pravda* liked the story so much that they ran it again ten years later.

At the time of our interrogation, the Russians had just put their first person in outer space. The interrogator said to me, "Look, we've had our spaceman up there, looking around, and we didn't find your God." After two days they were convinced that we were religious fanatics and not CIA operatives. With a submachine—gun guard, they escorted us to the Austrian border.

My goal, aim and desire was to get the Gospel into closed countries. We just went into one of the most closed countries on earth and promptly got kicked out. "What is God doing?" I wondered. I decided it was time to pray. I climbed a tree on a mountain in Austria to get alone so I could pray. I spent the day in prayer.

That day revolutionized my life and my ministry. God showed me that my vision was too small. He showed me that my job was to mobilize the church, and he wanted me to start with the European Church. It made sense, Europeans could drive to all kinds of closed countries. Americans, on the other hand, needed to cross the Atlantic before they could get to most of the countries they wanted to reach. The amount of money needed to get one American into a closed country could get two or three Europeans into the same place. Even after they got there, Europeans were usually better received than Americans.

Little did I know that this was to be the forerunner of a radical change that was to take place in mission thinking. This concept exploded from Europe to Asia and to Africa and then to Latin America. People from all different countries became equal partners in missions.

God gave me a name—the name that has stuck Operation Mobilisation—OM.

God also showed me how to mobilize the church—bringing people together for a summer, for two years and to send them on outreaches. Then sending them back to their home churches or to another mission agency to energize, revitalize the church and spread the vision.

That was 1961. Short-term mission trips were almost unheard of. It was a revolutionary concept, but it worked.

The next summer we recruited 200 volunteers. By the second summer in 1963, our group grew to 2,000, reaching 25 million people. We moved to London, where we assembled a fleet of 120 old trucks. We crossed the English Channel, split up into teams, and drove out to reach the unreached. Within a year of my arrest in the Soviet Union, we were sending Europeans back to the USSR who spoke fluent Russian and could accomplish more than I ever could.

We focused on getting into closed countries. That's why I sent Dale Rhoton to check out Afghanistan. "While you're in the neighborhood," I said, "you might as well check out Pakistan and India." I honestly didn't expect much to come from it. I knew missionaries were operating in West Pakistan, and I had already met vibrant Christians from India. Since India's strong churches were reaching India, I figured that country didn't need us. But Dale told me otherwise. "India needs us," he said.

So we sent two teams to India. They drove out to India in old trucks and encountered all kinds of problems getting there. I felt responsible, especially since I myself had recruited many of these team members. So in late 1963, I flew to India to see how things were going.

India shook me. I traveled around on trains, evangelizing and giving out tracts. I was blown away by the needs of the people in villages and towns. I said to my wife, "We are moving to India."

We lived in Bombay. People were drawn to our radical message about discipleship, forsaking all, world mission and prayer. Rather than feeling like we needed to import a foreign missionary every time we wanted to get something done, eventually we partnered with the church in India and supported nationals in ministry.

Our work exploded and then I got kicked out of the country. So we moved to Kathmandu as Indians could come to see me there without a visa. We specialized in leadership training and also started the work in Nepal.

Logistics were becoming a challenge. Driving old trucks back and forth across Europe and Asia wasn't working quite so well. As I prayed about this and looked at the globe, I was struck with how much water there is on the surface of the earth.

Then I felt we needed a ship!

When I shared the idea with the churches in Europe, some laughed. To some, owning a ship seemed like an extravagance. But the more I prayed about it, the more I was convinced that God wanted us to own a ship. I wanted a ship as soon as possible. Impatience, admittedly, is one of my failings, and God dealt with it by making me wait. We waited for six long years before our first ship, the 2,319-ton Logos set sail in 1971 from England to India.

In those days we didn't believe in fund raising. We thought we should follow the example of Hudson Taylor and George Müeller—never to make our needs publicly known, privately pray and trust God to supply.[3] When we signed a contract to purchase Umanak (which became the Logos 1), we had enough money to make a deposit, but not enough to complete the purchase. We prayed, God supplied, and by our deadline we had the exact amount to complete the purchase and have the ship towed to dry dock where it could be overhauled and painted.

---

[3]In recent years, we have come to believe that we should show our esteem for our partners in the local church by sharing our needs with them so they can join us in prayer and in giving.

Though it was exciting to finally have our ship, once we had it, the full reality of it began to sink in. In fact, we nearly shook with fear when we realized the dangers of the ship project—an old vessel, no insurance, all those young people aboard with their parents hovering anxiously in the background. I used to have nightmares about the ship going down, and would wake up thinking, "Let's keep it in the warmer climates, so that if it does sink at least the kids will have a chance. If you go down in cold seas, there's far less hope."[4]

Despite our anxieties, the ship ministry became more than we ever expected. We acquired a second, larger ship (the Doulos), and the two became floating bookstores and literature centers, as well as launching pads for short-term missions. Staffed by 400 volunteers from 40–50 nations, our ships have visited ports all over the world from India to Jamaica and from Egypt to Communist China.

Operation Mobilisation has grown to 4,000 full-time staff plus another 3,000–4,000 short-term people during any one year. 130,000 people have been trained in OM representing many denominations. Over 100 mission agencies trace their birth to their founders or leaders being in OM. Our literature ministry, Send the Light (STL), in the UK is now a separate ministry with 600 employees and 40 bookstores. We are in over 100 countries, including most of the difficult and limited access nations across the world. We have become a much more holistic ministry. In the last ten years, we have put flesh and bone on the compassion of Jesus by reaching out to victims of earthquakes, floods, war and poverty—meeting physical as well as spiritual needs.

This growth has been a direct and exhilarating answer to prayer. No one accomplishes anything without God. And we certainly did not get into closed countries without a lot of prayer. We've also seen

---

[4] George Verwer, *No Turning Back*, OM Lit., Waynesboro, GA, USA, pp. 70–71.

personal answers to prayer. My wife's father was killed in World War II. Her stepfather asked her to leave home because he was anti-Christian. Yet, after 25 years of prayer, he came to Christ.

At Moody we were known as the group that was always praying. This was back in the late 1950's when praying in small groups was unheard of. While I'm sure others were birthing this practice of praying in small groups at the same time, this approach has spread like a phenomenon all over the world. Now it's part of our culture. In 1958 we started the practice of meeting for a half night in prayer—a practice that has continued for forty-three years.

I believe in and practice prayer. I believe God answers prayer. Yet unanswered or seemingly unanswered prayer is one of the great altars upon which God makes true men and women. My life is full of unanswered prayers. Not even 50 percent of my prayers have been answered not yet at least.[5]

I aim high as I believe in a great and powerful God. When my hopes, dreams and prayers are not realized, I get discouraged. In fact, all my life I have struggled with discouragement. But I stand on the promises of God. I have determined to never let the sun go down on my discouragement. That can be a challenge.

We have certainly faced difficult times. Just before midnight on January 4, 1988, the Logos struck a rock in the Beagle Channel at the southern tip of South America. All 139 persons aboard (including a six-month-old baby), were evacuated, and the ship went down.

On the evening of August 10, 1991, two young OM workers were killed when terrorists threw a grenade into a meeting, we were holding in Zamboanga, Philippines. An OM worker was kidnapped by Afghans and never heard from him again. Another worker was shot in Turkey. I don't know why these things happened. There is a mystery in suffering that we will never fully understand.

---

[5]George Verwer, *No Turning Back,* OM Lit., Waynesboro, GA, USA, p. 104.

I'm not the same person I was in 1960. Yes, I am still eager to share the gospel, but God has had to change me and change my ideas. Many of us trained in Bible school back in the 1950's had a Pharisee streak—a grace-killing streak. Our ideas about money, prayer and evangelism and our man-made rules became the measuring line of how spiritual we were. We were judgmental, even when we tried not to be, our body language gave us away.

I was so focused, so zealous, so determined that I used to walk right by people without acknowledging them. Many times I was too hard on my wife. God confronted me about this, even from the very first month of our marriage when I hurt my wife and I saw her sitting and crying. God used the ministry of men like Oswald J. Smith and Roy Hession to bring me back, weeping, to the cross.

God showed me that 1 Corinthians 13 (the *Love* chapter) was for us, the most important chapter in the Bible. Though I believe in world missions and radical commitment, these things mean nothing if we don't have Christ's love.

We need big heartedness. We need what Charles Swindoll calls a "grace awakening." We need balanced, consistent Christianity.

Chapter 6

Urbana 1968

(A message that George gave at Urbana, a large
student missions event in 1968)

I do not think I can explain to you how difficult it is for me to speak. I have never spoken in conventions like this in my life. I have been out of America for almost eight years, except for a few weeks traveling to Mexico. Most of my life and time have been given to personal counseling and personal evangelism. So if you think that I am not serious in what I say, I can only ask you to somehow give me a chance to know you personally. I would do almost anything tonight to help at least one needy person in this auditorium.

I know of some young people who, when reading a missionary biography, only become depressed. I know some who, when reading the story of the men who were martyred in South America many years ago, only become convinced that they will never make it. They read about George Müeller and how he prayed for millions of Pounds to support his orphanages by faith, and they do not even understand it and become overwhelmed. I think if I had been sitting here as a freshman in college (I had been a Christian only one year at that time), hearing some of these challenges and facts and the qualifications so tremendously presented by our brethren, I have to confess that I couldn't have done it.

Some of you already have come to me with your problems. Many of you have admitted and spoken among yourselves about the dichotomy I spoke about in an earlier message, and you know it is very real. My heart goes out to you who are sons and daughters of missionaries, Christians and strong evangelicals; to you who have been raised from a very early age like my own children on Bible verses. My son at six years passed out hundreds of tracts by himself in a single day. And perhaps some of you were doing the same thing as young children. Yet now at university or at college somehow it is not real any longer.

I admit that I am preaching for a decision on your part tonight as I believe Jesus Christ preached on the part of his hearers. He told Zacchaeus to come down. He told the blind man to put mud on his eyes. Wherever he went, he called people to make decisions.

However, it is with fear that I would call anyone to make a decision without counting the cost. I think of the words in Luke 14 where Jesus said that we must count the cost. Before you make a decision like this, before you sign your name for something like this, you must count the cost lest you become like thousands of young people (those of us on the platform know this is true) who have signed their names, who have raised their hands, yet who have never fulfilled that commitment.

Yes, I am afraid if I had been here as a freshman, I would have been somewhat frustrated. We speak about these qualifications. Who can live like this? Recently I was reading Andrew Murray's book on humility and it made me want to quit the ministry! I could not even understand what Murray was talking about, much less ever have it. Time and again as I read books by men of God and study biographies, I have felt so overwhelmed by it all—by the responsibility of the Christian life.

I want to speak especially to those of you who feel somewhat overwhelmed, somewhat incapable. You have problems in your life. You know that this dichotomy is very real for you, and though you sing "Onward Christian Soldiers," you have never marched for Christ. Though you sing, "Who Will Follow in His Train?" you know deep in your heart you are not following in his train. The hymns that we have sung even in these meetings, carry enough spiritual truth to drive us to the uttermost parts of the earth, and to the unconverted people in our universities—our commitment is real.

If the statements on this card become real in our lives, we would become revolutionists for Jesus Christ. People would be won on our campuses. Our Christian unions would become alive by the love of Jesus Christ. We would be constrained to go, to give, to love, and to experience the tremendous reality that is in Jesus Christ. An atheist once said to an evangelical Christian in the British Isles: "If I believed what you say you believe, I would cross Britain upon my knees on broken glass to tell men about it."

When I graduated from my high school I was called the class clown. Everything was a joke to me. I had more jokes, witty stories, swear words and things to keep people laughing all night. I always got excited or suddenly interested when a meeting ended early— because my Saturday nights used to begin about ten. We would go over the river into New York City with one of our girls—I had about thirty-two of them when I was between twelve and sixteen years old. (Don't laugh—some of you have had far more than that.) We would begin to dance old-fashioned rock and roll. (The Twist was just coming in when I got twisted out by the Lord. Praise be to God.) I had loud speakers all over my room that automatically kicked on in the mornings and roused me out of bed to jazz or something else. I lived on music. We would start about 10:00p.m. and I loved it.

When Jesus Christ found me I could not say I was sad. I was fantastically happy. I had a beautiful blond next to me in the seat at Madison Square Garden. I was enjoying life. Some people think you come to Christ only when you are sad, overwhelmed, depressed, or have a tremendous guilt complex.

No, not necessarily. I want to say this with all my heart: God pulled me out of night clubs and he gave me something more real or I would never be here. I loved dance, music, and all the things of the world. Even today if somebody played a juke box in the corner I would have to hold my knees still. But for the past nine years the only thing that had kept me up as late as a prom night—and it has been every other week or so—is spending a night with believers in prayer and worship to God, spending seven or eight hours in the presence of God and in worship to him.

God is real. I want to tell you that God is so real that, though my friends said I would be back in one month, I have not been back once in eleven years. I want to tell you that God is so real, he can make Rock and Roll and all the poison, sugar-coated pills of this world seem like dead stones in the middle of a desert. I am convinced that Jesus Christ is so real, his love is so tremendous, that when we really fall in love with him and really experience his life, the things of this world fall off without the ninety-nine negatives that are often preached at us.

Many of you may think that God is not that real to you. You say, "Well, that's okay for you. God found you in a nightclub. But what about us—Christian young people?"

I want to tell you about one of my best friends. Jonathan was a student leader at Moody Bible Institute when I was a student. He met me in the Student Council. Jonathan was born on the mission field and raised by missionary parents. Jonathan once told me he had never kissed a girl in his life. I told him that I would not take a girl on a date if I could not. . .(never mind the word I used). But I could not believe a fellow could be like Jonathan. And from his very early years on a mission field Jonathan has, to this day, gone on for God. There was a time when his commitment became very unreal. There was a time when he almost became an agnostic, even in the middle of Bible school program. But as he met other Christians, as he experienced reality and saw that Christianity could be lived, that Jesus Christ is alive in the 20th century, he recommitted his life to God and has become a mighty man for God. It is only because of Jonathan that I have been able to go to Asia, because he coordinates our work all over Europe. He has the same life, the same zeal; he has more love and more reality than I do. Yet he came from a home just like many of you.

Jesus Christ can meet every need. Whether God found you in the deepest ditch in Chicago or as a missionary child, he can meet your need tonight.

There are needs here—needs in the social life. Billy Graham, in his book, *World Aflame,* says we are a nation of sex gluttons. It is true. This is the biggest battle of your life on campus. Billy said in the 1957 convention, "And if you do not win this battle, you are going to lose all around." I am convinced that Jesus Christ is sufficient for your sex battles, wherever and whatever they may be. I pray you will take some of the Inter-Varsity books on this subject and devour them. But what they say will only be a reality in your life, as you experience the sufficiency of Jesus Christ to meet your emotional longings.

When he meets your need, when you experience victory and know reality, then and only then can you be God's man and God's woman on the mission field.

I am not talking about perfection. I have not come to offer you any kind of spiritual pep pill. I did not say, "Believe this, and everything from now on will be perfect." No! Jesus Christ said, "If any man would come after me, let him deny himself and take up his cross and follow me." Do you believe that? He repeatedly said that in each of the Gospels.

There will be struggles and battles. Victory is not easy, but there is victory. The Book of 1 John says, "This is the victory that overcomes the world, even our faith."

In a few minutes, though I do not like it and my personality rebels against it, I am going to give you the opportunity to express faith like Zacchaeus' when he came down from the tree. You are going to be thinking about it in these next few minutes.

My invitation to you is not necessarily to become a missionary. You have to work out what and where you are on your knees before God. I do not believe that we as so-called missionaries are necessarily any more committed than the person who never moves out of his place. I believe that with all my heart. If God calls you to a carpenter shop, remember Jesus was a carpenter most of the years of his life. As you work out your vocation and location and prayerfully seek God's will (and that is one of the great privileges we have—to know the will of God) you can fill out the card with sincerity and faith.

My invitation is to those of you who want to know reality in your life at any cost. Maybe during these days at the conference something has been ringing in your heart. I cannot explain it to you. It will be as unique in one man as it is in another.

The decision for one might be to know Jesus Christ, maybe you do not know Christ. Maybe you came here believing you were a Christian, and now the Spirit of God has witnessed to you and you realize, you have never been born again. I have known people going door to door with our movement to distribute Christian literature or testify personally for Christ, who discovered they did not know him—and they were converted on the door step!

Some here already have confessed faith in Jesus Christ. But my main invitation and appeal to you—and I appeal to your logic more than to anything else—is that you will come to the end of yourself. I pray that you will be honest and admit that you do not have reality in your heart and the Lord convicts you about it. You may admit that the dichotomy exists—that, what you say you are, is not really operational and real in your life.

All of the reality will not come in one night, but there has to be a beginning. I believe that there has to be some kind of crisis in each person's life. Most people experience many crises in their lives for God. I think the idea that there is only one special spiritual crisis for a person, is one of the biggest lies Satan can ever get us to believe. The men of God whom I have studied have had all different kinds of crises, and some have had many. But in all instances their crises were followed by a process each. If you are not ready for the process, to place importance on your quiet time, then do not stand to your feet tonight.

If you are not serious about Bible study, if you are not enthusiastic to get into God's Word and let it devour you, then you are not ready. You see, our problems are in our unconscious mind. The dichotomy of our life is rooted in our unconscious mind. We do things we do not want to do. We say things we do not want to say. They just come because those deep problems surge up from our background, and our childhood. We wonder, "Why did I say that? Why did I do that?" I believe one of the areas for the cleansing power of the Word of God is in the unconscious mind, that is why you must be serious about Bible study.

You say, "But I don't have time to get into the Word at the university!" During my first year at university I did not know how I would ever get any time for Bible study as I was running back and forth across the campus. But the only way I got through all of the courses I took, including Bible teaching from unbelieving professors, was through spending hours on my knees.

I asked a Ph.D. holder from Princeton, "How did you get through Princeton University and still remain a tower of strength preaching the full gospel of the Lord Jesus Christ?" He said, "Young man, I spent two hours every day on my knees, studying the Word of God."

You have to find time to get into the Word of God and you will find it. I prayed, "God, give me time" and he did.

My Physics teacher lectured about everything but Physics. So I took my Physics book and covered it with memory verses, hundreds of Bible verses that God put in my thick skull by his grace, and this revolutionized my thinking.

I am sorry to confess that at the age of sixteen I began, among other things, to peddle pornographic literature. My unconscious and conscious mind was warped by the pornographic filth that pours out in our country. But I can confess today that because of the power of the Word of God I have a new mind. I want to tell you it is a liberty, and freedom beyond anything you can ever experience. That which Jesus Christ can give, I believe, makes drugs seem like a useless pill, to say the least.

Oh, young people, do you think I am just saying this? If so, will you ask the hundreds of young people from all over the world who have worked and lived with me? The only reason these young people—Cambridge and Oxford men, Swedish people, and all the rest—have stuck it out is because in their lives and minds—God is real. Men can actually live like the Lord Jesus Christ in the 20th and 21st century. There will be failures, sin, and violence, but God is real. Victory can be yours if you love Jesus and if you want it.

I want to speak for a few moments to the women. I wish my wife was here. Maybe you think I am burning all out for Christ because I have a fanatic wife. Well, my wife could not be more human.

To begin with, she had everything against her. She is from a broken home. Her father was killed in Germany and she had to leave home and live in an orphanage as a small girl. She had the major human problem: She wanted love. She wanted marriage, because she thought that everything would be settled if only she were married. I know many girls here tonight are like that. You would not dare think of going to the mission field single.

My wife was converted before I met her, but that had not solved all her problems. That was only the beginning. (The Bible says that the new birth is only the beginning. If only we would realize that!) After we met and had fallen in love we got to know each other and to my surprise I discovered she had some serious problems.

My wife's problems were three psychosomatic illnesses: migraine headaches, back tension pain, and heartaches. (Doctors say 50 percent of our illnesses are due to psychosomatic causes.) With such physical problems, my wife could not go to the mission field. She went to Mexico with one of our teams, and was in bed every night in tears and every kind of problem you could possibly dream of. When we got back, she tried to get help from a book, *Health Springs Forth,* but her problems remained.

So we knew we had to part. I had to go to the mission field. We sat in the lobby of our school one night, and I told her that though I loved her with all my heart, we would have to break it off. That could have destroyed her because she wanted to marry me more than anything else in life. This was the one thing she had hoped for. Her sickness got worse. She went to her room and did what everybody told her to do—"cast it on the Lord." But she picked up her pain the next morning and carried it all day.

At the end of the fourth day she realized the greatest truth in the Bible—that Jesus Christ is an all-sufficient Savior. He is sufficient for all our needs—for our emotional problems, and intellectual problems. There in her room, in complete quiet, she bowed down before God (as I am going to ask some of you to do tonight) and said, "Lord, I believe that you are my victory. I believe that you are all that I need. I am ready to go to the mission field without George Verwer."

Peace and joy flooded her heart and she was miraculously healed of all her sicknesses. She has been pioneering on for Jesus Christ in difficult circumstances all over the world since then.

People say, "Be careful," and I am sure even tonight some are saying, "Watch out! this commitment business is just emotion." It is amazing—we can get emotional about anything and nobody says a thing. I used to come home at six o'clock in the morning, singing, shouting, doing all kinds of activities. I was the craziest one in the school. I would get out on the football field and shout and play the drums and do anything in the football game—and they elected me Student Body President.

But if you begin to shout for Christ, if you have an emotional experience with the Lord in which he becomes real to you and you express your love for him, people will call you fanatic and say, "Be careful, the emotion will wear off." That is what they told me the night I accepted Christ in the Billy Graham meeting. But the emotion does not wear off if it is followed up by continual interaction with the Holy Spirit of God.

I could tell you stories about Communists in London, girls from the back streets of Paris, boys from the Hindu temples of southern India, young men who have taken bottles of strong poison to kill themselves before they found the living Christ in reality—I could give example after example.

Christianity is real, young people, but I believe with all my heart it is real only to those who come to the place where they say, "Lord Jesus, you are all I want." It cannot be Jesus plus this or that, not even Jesus plus evangelism. With me, it could not be Jesus plus Operation Mobilisation. It has to be Jesus Christ and him alone.

I am convinced that if you are willing to come to the end of yourself and say, "Lord Jesus, you are all I want," then God will begin to break that dichotomy and you will begin to experience a reality that you have never known in your Christian life. I know this is true. I pray that you will consider it, and act as God leads you.

In Colossians 2:9–10, we read, *In him* (Jesus Christ) *the whole fulness of deity dwells bodily, and you have come to fulness of life in him, who is the head of all rule and authority* (RSV). Please, young people, consider Jesus Christ who can give you fullness of life—not a dichotomy, not two people—a whole person in him. Tonight, come to that place where you say, "Lord Jesus Christ, you are my all. You are my everything. I will follow you. I will do whatever you want me to do."

Chapter 7

Seven Major Emphases

Operation Mobilisation is a Christian Fellowship of learners moving out to the frontiers of world evangelization. The movement is both international and interdenominational. It is a fellowship specializing in evangelistic and discipleship training for young people. This training is carried out through working together on teams on the field or in our various headquarters. Our young people are involved in many methods of evangelism, with a special emphasis on the use of literature as a tool for both teaching believers and reaching the masses with the gospel. We desire to be disciples of Christ, learning and teaching what is on the heart of God as we find it in his Word, the Bible.

Here are seven of our deepest and strongest convictions. We desire, above all else, to put these into practice in our own lives, while at the same time sharing them with others as God gives the opportunity.

1. Worship and Prayer
Our worship is more important than our work and any act of

sacrifice. Worship is adoring and praising God for who he is. Worship and evangelism should be the spontaneous outflow of a life in communion with God. Worship is the foundation for the many other aspects of prayer, which is so basic to spiritual life and to accomplishing God's purposes.

A.W. Tozer said that worship was "the missing jewel of the evangelical church" and we now long to see that jewel put back into its rightful place. It is one thing to talk about worship and to acknowledge its importance. It is quite another to know the reality of worship in our day-by-day living and team efforts. This means that we must be disciplined in giving time to worship, praise, and to all forms of prayer, especially intercession.

2. Love and Forgiveness

The importance of love and forgiveness is the easiest message to pay lip service to in the church today. I believe that it is impossible to overemphasize love, especially when the message is based on truth. Love and truth together produce the kind of spiritual balance we desperately need. This is one of the reasons why we published the book, *The Revolution of Love*, which is available in many languages and has brought an amazing response. As we move forward in the spiritual warfare, our motivation is not based on legalistic regulations or attempting to prove ourselves. It is based on the love of God and the forgiveness we have in Jesus Christ.

Grace is a key word and a basic principle in everything that we do. This must be a major emphasis in every aspect of our work. All of us should memorize I Corinthians 13 and always remember that love is flexible, adaptable, and must be central. God's Word tells us in 1 John that if we cannot love those whom we have seen, we cannot love him, our great God, whom we have not seen. Jesus adds to this teaching by saying that if we love him, we will keep his commandments.

3. Victorious Living and the Holy Spirit's Fullness

We believe that there is a victorious lifestyle, a lifestyle of Spirit-filled and Spirit-controlled living, this includes what to do when we sin (1 John 2:1). This is not super-spirituality; it is total reality.

Various parts of the New Testament emphasize the victorious life in different ways. As Jesus taught in all the Gospels, it means denying self, taking up the cross, and following him. As outlined in Hebrews 4, it involves a "rest of faith" in which the Holy Spirit is working in and through us. While we believe strongly in distributing outstanding literature and messages on CD, video and film, presenting the way of victory and spiritual power, we want to make every effort to avoid extremism, and show the various aspects of spiritual balance. We are aware that what A.W. Tozer said is often true, "The more keen Christian is more easily led astray."

We don't want to argue over the different expressions and vocabulary in regard to this great life in Christ, for we understand that God works in different ways in different people. We realize that this reality comes sometimes by crisis, but that the crisis must be followed by a process. The Spirit-filled life is not the end, but the beginning. It means that we constantly walk with Jesus with a learning spirit; always growing and always pressing on to higher avenues and higher plateaus in the things of the Spirit.

4. Christ's Lordship and All-Sufficiency

This is one of the most liberating and powerful aspects of the message that God has put on our hearts. We have seen thousands of people changed when they have really come to appropriate what belongs to them in Jesus Christ; and then, on a day-by-day basis make him Lord of their lives. Jesus Christ must be King, and this means that self must be put out of power. We must understand that many of God's people are discouraged and defeated. What we need is not another series of legalisms, "do this or do that," but we need the revolutionary life of our Lord Jesus Christ. We need Jesus himself, not just policies or even principles. It is fine to be able to testify about what Jesus did in our lives ten years ago, but what has happened since then? What is Jesus doing this week or today? We must communicate to others by our lives the transforming power of our Lord Jesus Christ, and we believe this will encourage others to come into this way of life, which of course, begins at conversion.

5. Honesty and True Openness

Honesty and openness are desperately needed among God's people today. We must take off our masks and face reality about ourselves. Billy Graham said that the greatest obstacle to our sanctification is our unwillingness to see ourselves as we really are. At the same time, we do not dwell either on ourselves or our past sins—the ones for which we have repented and brought under the forgiving power in the blood of Jesus, but we press forward with our eyes on the Savior, not ourselves. We must avoid, like the plague, any form of double living. We must allow the Spirit of God to deal with the sins of our disposition as well as our attitudes. For indeed, walking in the light of God's truth means all-out warfare against sin, Satan, and self. As sin is acknowledged and confessed, and relationships are restored, homes and churches will be revived and healed.

6. Discipline and Brokenness

Andrew Murray said that brokenness was humility's response to the touch of God. We must always be willing to take correction, from the Lord and also from others. We then must be willing to follow through in learning the reality of self-discipline in every area of our lives. We are aware that this is a long, hard road. If Paul had to say, "I buffet my body and bring it into subjection lest after preaching to others I become a reprobate," how much more do we need to know this kind of discipline!

Today churches and Christian organizations are desperate for disciplined people who can also assume important God-given responsibilities of leadership. The Holy Spirit will work in different ways in different lives not only bringing this discipline to pass, but in its outworking on a daily basis.

Truly effective discipline is always linked with a realization of God's sovereignty. We are weak, make mistakes, and fall into sin, but God has ultimate control over every situation. We must always keep this in mind as we press forward in the spiritual warfare, holding high the shield of faith.

7. World Evangelization

We believe emphatically, uncompromisingly, and without apology in world evangelization; in obedience to the clear teachings of the Lord Jesus Christ, in the Gospels and also in Acts 1:8, just before he ascended into heaven. World evangelization must be an international operation of all believers—especially moving forward to reach the unevangelized areas. We must not be side-tracked by controversy, but rather press forward, united together on basic biblical doctrines and the fundamental principles of the New Testament.

In some areas of the world we will work in depth, remaining there for many decades. In other areas we will have a catalyst ministry. We believe this will light fires which will burn in the hearts of individuals and then churches to accomplish the great task of world evangelization. Let us never forget that great promise in Galatians: *Let us not be weary in well doing: . . .we shall reap, if we faint not* (6:9).

If these are the basic principles with which you agree, and which you want to make the basic goals in your life, then we want to unite together with you in prayer and in practical work as much as possible to accomplish this task together.

Note: I wrote this article almost 40 years ago and I am happy to say that these 7 Emphases are still a vital part of OM though not always expressed in the same way. The main thing I would add today would be our emphasis on the whole person and the marriage between social concern and action with all other forms of evangelism.

Chapter 8

 A Few More Convictions

Peter Maiden has asked me to share a few final words as I was stepping down as International Coordinator of Operation Mobilisation. Here are seven terms I would like to give you.

1. Faithfulness

God has been so faithful! I have experienced that every day since my conversion. We can trust him 100 percent for the future. He never promised an easy road.

2. Thanksgiving

I want to thank all OMers, exOMers, prayer partners and supporters for their vital part in all that God has done. I want to thank local churches and other agencies for their love, loyalty and patience. Let's remember 1 Thessalonians 5:18.

3. Forgiveness

I thank God for his great forgiveness to me, and also all people, on any occasion, as they forgave me and allowed love to cover my wrongdoing. It is my prayer that God will take the "revolution of love" and forgiveness much deeper into the DNA of the Movement.

4. Change
How I thank God for the wisdom and grace he gave us to keep growing and to keep changing! In the process, we have made mistakes and he has been merciful. The OM of 2003 is not the same OM of the sixties, but we have held fast to the basics, especially concerning God's Word and the Lord Jesus.

5. Purity
I believe, the challenge of moral purity linked with integrity will be one of the biggest challenges in the years to come. We need to take serious steps to maintain this. Our willingness to humble ourselves and stay accountable will be key in this area of the battle.

6. Unity
If you listen to the old orientation tapes, you will realize how much love and unity were emphasized from the earliest days. One of the greatest encouragements over these 45 years is to see how this has been maintained, not in the absence of sin and failure, but in the midst of it. The message of *The Calvary Road* and other similar books has had a huge impact. Our unity will be tested in new (and old) ways in the future and I pray that we will stand firm in the grace that is in Christ Jesus.

7. Faith
We live in very troubled times. As I write this, the war in Iraq is going in full force and the level of fear and hatred is growing at a phenomenal rate. The kind of work we are doing, with all its variety, may become more difficult. This may also increase the level of misunderstanding among us.

Our faith is going to be tested. Let's focus on Ephesians 6:16, taking hold of the shield of faith. The unique system God has given, so that we can see our own support come in, has some negative factors, but I believe the positives outweigh them 10 to 1.

I thank God for how the transition has gone, and I stand 100 percent with Peter Maiden, Joseph D'souza and Francois Vosloo and all the area and field leaders as they move forward. Drena and I look forward with faith and joy to our new roles. Thank you for your prayers.

Chapter 9

Seven Global Scourges

I have been sharing a lot on the story of the Good Samaritan. Let's look at Luke 10 beginning at verse 25. Jesus often told stories to communicate a truth. In our day we try to give an answer, even if we don't really know the answer. Jesus, the Son of the living God often answered with a question. In verse 30, Jesus replied with an illustration: "A (Jewish) man was traveling from Jerusalem to Jericho and was attacked by bandits who robbed him of his clothes and money. They beat him up and left him half-dead by the side of the road." Wow! A friend of mine from Nigeria had almost an identical experience, this is happening even today, so this is relevant.

"By chance a (Jewish) priest came along and when he saw the man lying there he crossed to the other side of the road and passed him by." This seems incredible doesn't it? How can a man just pass by someone who is beaten up and lying on the side of the road? "Then the temple assistant came along and also passed by on the other side of the road." What a sad and pathetic situation! "Then a despised Samaritan came along and when he saw the man he felt deep pity for him. Kneeling beside him, the Samaritan helped him." Samaritans were considered enemies of the Jews and were considered to be like scum. They were the people down the road with whom the Jews had no dealings with, like a *Dalit* or an "Untouchable" in India.

So this despised Samaritan comes along, kneels down, bandages the man and puts him on his donkey and takes him to an Inn where he could be taken care of. The next day he gives the innkeeper two pieces of silver and tells him to take care of him. The innkeeper is assured, if the bill runs higher, then he will be paid the difference next time he passes through. What a powerful and revolutionary story!

The story of the Good Samaritan is a favorite story of children. As adults, we sometimes just gloss over and read the story. What we need to understand is that Jesus, after he told this story, asked the question, "Now which of these three men was a neighbor to the man who was attacked by the bandits?" The man replied, picking up at verse 36, "The one who showed mercy." Then Jesus said, "Yes, now go and do the same." If only he had not said that! This is a great challenge when it says clearly, "yes," now go and do the same. We have to start doing some thinking.

I have made many mistakes in my Christian life and God has been very merciful. We can't possibly learn all the lessons in God's Word just in a year or even 10 years. When I first launched into ministry I was not that concerned about peoples' physical needs in terms of my own ministry. I prayed for people often if they were ill and was concerned in my heart, but I made the mistake of thinking that other organizations like World Vision or Tear Fund, medical missionaries, agencies like the Salvation Army and later on people like Mother Theresa—they answered the Good Samaritan call and it was their ministry. My ministry was literature evangelism, winning people to Christ, training people, planting churches and leadership. We were overwhelmed with what we were attempting to do, much less take on other tasks in terms of peoples' physical needs. That was a great mistake on our part. It took people from the two-thirds of the world and people like Tony Campolo and Samuel Escobar, men and women from many different countries, a deeper study of the Word of God and a re-look at stories like the Good Samaritan to completely change me in regard to this great challenge.

There are many people today lying by the side of the road. We cannot pass them by, nor can we just give them a tract or a Bible and say, "See you later." We must somehow respond to the challenge of Jesus concerning peoples' physical situation. If you are already overcommitted, this message needs to be contextualized into your situation; I am not wanting you to just take on more in terms of deeds and action, but I want you to take this message into your heart and your spiritual DNA and share it with others who may not be overcommitted, and not yet even be saved.

This aspect of our kingdom message appeals to non-Christians. Many non-Christians are the pace setters in some of the things I am going to talk about. When we, maybe not even fully understanding it, at least sympathize with them and have some discernment (Christians often lack discernment in these areas) we are going to find them more open to talk about Jesus. Britain is one of the most humanitarian nations that has existed in history. It is part of the culture and DNA of the nation. Even as the nation has tended to part and leave the basics of the Christian faith, the challenge of giving has remained within the culture. All different charities are trying to raise money. You and I, if we want to make an impact in post-modern Britain, have to learn to affirm people who as yet don't know Jesus, but are doing good things rather than constantly come across negative about anyone who is not a Christian. The amount of prejudice against Christians today is greater than it had been before, for many reasons, rather than get very upset and blame this person or that person, especially those in government, we need Holy Ghost's discernment to understand the new culture in which we live.

There are inumerable global scourges around us, but let me list here just seven. What I am talking here is not about individuals, but clusters of people.

1. Children at Risk

The first person lying by the side of the road is a little child of millions of little children. One billion children are at risk, about one-sixth of the earth's population. Many of them are dying. Many groups in the world are responding to "children at risk," but research by Viva Network and Patrick McDonald has shown that there is an awful lot of work yet to be done. We are speaking of children who are sold into factory slavery, and thousands of children in age of 11 or 12 are sold into sexual slavery. We are talking about street children in places like Brazil, where sometimes even the police pull the trigger and murder them. We are talking about millions of AIDS orphans in Africa and other countries.

There are new books coming out about children, some of them are living right down the street, sometimes abused by their own parents. If you do not think that is an issue then you are living in a cloud and you need to come down to earth. If you don't think that happens to those who profess to be followers of Jesus Christ, then you obviously have not been involved in much personal ministry with people. "Children at risk" is overwhelming and it is time for the church to speak out and to reach out and do what the Good Samaritan did in Luke 10.

2. Abused Women

The second person lying by the side of the road is a woman, an abused woman, a woman at risk. *True Grit* by Debbie Meroff, I believe, is probably the most significant book that we have ever published by Authentic Media. This is a book about women and what they are suffering. We have reprinted this book many times over by now. It is unbelievable to know what is going on in Europe in the area of sex trafficking; even President Bush has been speaking out about this, as well as other global leaders. We need to have a more biblical, revolutionary view of women and their suffering. The abuse of women under certain religious systems is unbelievable. What went on in Afghanistan during the Taliban rule? Very few Christians spoke out about it. The Feminist Movement, they have many positive and negative points, were the first to speak out on the suffering of women in Afghanistan. In God's mercy the Taliban was removed. What about female circumcision? Have you ever read anything about that or do you prefer not to read things that are unpleasant?

Friend, let me tell you something, if you do not want to read things that are unpleasant, then whatever you do, don't read the Bible. Some of the most unpleasant stories I have ever read, including rape, are written in the Bible. I believe one of the marks of authenticity of the Word of God is that it does not gloss over sin even when it is committed by a great leader like David, a man after God's own heart, who was guilty of murder and adultery.

You and I need to speak out about things like female circumcision. I think the Danish Government was the first to want to get a law against this. I can read pretty heavy stuff without getting ill, but I have never been able to finish what I have attempted to read about female circumcision, it is so sickening. It is so disturbing that women could be so abused and it is growing and still going on. Hundreds of thousands of women are going through this unbelievable ordeal.

3. The Extreme Poor

The third person lying by the side of the road is, what we call, the extreme poor. There are many poor people, and it is sad that many christians with just one cliché write the whole thing off, even misquoting from the New Testament. If we study the Bible and listen to men and women of God down through the years going right back to William Booth, we know that God has a bias towards the poor. Some of you come from a poor background, and you should never ever be ashamed of that. You should never feel inferior in this society that is still a class and racist and "caste"ist society even though we do not like to admit it. Some of the greatest people in the world came from the poorest background and some are still poor.

What about the Dalits of India known as the Untouchables? There are 250 million of them which is more than three times the population of the British Isles. In the past few years the Dalits have started to move, they are leaving Hinduism by the thousands. Many have become Buddhists while others are knocking at the door of the church. In OM alone we have planted over two thousand churches in the last couple of years mainly for Dalits and many are experiencing the reality of the Holy Spirit. It is an incredible thing that we have experienced in our Movement and we were almost 50 years in the trenches. In India we have decided to be involved with the extreme disenfranchised and poor under the leadership of Joseph D'souza (he has written a book about the Dalits). We decided to become involved in human rights, not in every aspect because it is such a huge area and no one can easily get beyond their boundaries. A new movement (All India Christian Council) was born with Joseph D'souza, the leader of OM India, who was made the head of the Board. It is separate from OM, with all different agencies and churches, mainly Bible-believing people, to speak out in connection with the persecution of Christians in India, (especially after Graham Staines and his two sons were murdered) and the cause of the Dalits.

Human rights: concern for human rights and defense of human rights are a part of God's kingdom. Guess what? Most Christians who are not involved with human rights still believe in it, because they get really upset when one of their neighbors does something that is a breech of their human rights. I am amazed at what upsets the average person. It is usually trivial, but often is connected with human rights without us realizing it. We all believe in justice and human rights. It took me years to grasp this, but we are not just called to evangelize the world; we are also called to build the kingdom everywhere. That is overwhelming and you have to find your place and get guidance. If you can capture the whole vision in your heart that will enable you to respond better to your particular part of the vision, no matter how small that may be. The global poor should be a priority and there is much that we can do. The church, more than ever before in history, is responding to this challenge. The story of Tear Fund is one of the greatest Christian stories in the British Isles as is the story of Bob Pearce founding World Vision and then Samaritan's Purse and hundreds of other smaller less known agencies around the globe.

4. People with HIV/AIDS

The fourth person lying by the side of the road is the person with HIV/AIDs. Forty million have been infected and 20 million have died. Millions of children have been orphaned and whole societies are burgeoning under the weight of so many dying so young. Rather than standing by and judging, let us respond in love and action. (Many have HIV and don't know it.) Let us also take advantage of this opportunity to share the gospel. We have found that, because death is so imminent, AIDS patients are very open to the gospel. I would urge you to read *Aids and You* by Patrick Dixon. It is being supplied free around the globe. I took Patrick to meet with 50 Africans and others in Uganda who were concerned about this huge pandemic and it is overwhelming when we think of the task. The church is on the move. There is a great lack of finance in this battle. In the western world you can get expensive medical cocktails, so people can live another five or ten years, but so many in India and

Africa do not have access to these medications and medicines. We know of a few cases where God has intervened and healed people. I don't believe that we should limit our response to that huge problem only through prayer, though prayer has got to be a part of it. God sometimes does unusual things. We must respond in the mobilization of the entire church for prevention. In Africa almost every church has people in their congregation with HIV/AIDS. It is uncanny, many of these people do not die of AIDS, you don't die of AIDS. AIDS runs your body down so that any one of 50 different illnesses takes you in the end. Many die very young.

5. People without Clean Water

The fifth person lying by the side of the road is the thirsty person. Water is becoming increasingly scarce. Thirty percent of the world has no access to clean water. Many must walk miles to get clean water, and so often the ones who do it are children whose bodies are not designed for such back-breaking work. Big cities are running out of water and are shipping it in at great cost, while in other parts of the world the dysfunctional water systems are breeding grounds for disease. May each of us be part of the effort to see more people getting clean water, as we seek to preserve the precious water at our disposal.

My issue is the people in poverty-stricken areas of the world where there is drought and other difficulties leading to no access to pure water. They drink impure water from the river and many of them will be dead within the year. You and I can do something about it. Christian agencies are being raised up that primarily deal with getting pure water. Non-Christians are doing it as well. Would you pray for these people? Would you pray for the release of money because it takes money to drill wells, and to make a water-purifying-machine from very basic components. It is incredible what can be done when we exercise a little sanctified imagination. That has always been one of my prayers for God's chosen frozen—a little more sanctified imagination. If you are one of these basic boring Christians, let me tell you there is still hope for you, don't give up. Even if you are my age, there is still hope that a fire would be lit in your heart. Let us serve the thirsty people, the sick people, with simple pure water.

6. The Environment

The sixth person lying by the side of the road, this is going to really surprise you, is the planet earth, the environment. I was reading sitting in a train, and a man sitting behind me asked, "Are you George Verwer?" We talked and I discovered he was a Christian from Sunderland. He had heard me preach in Dublin in the seventies and somehow it struck a cord in his heart. He shared how his work is in connection with the environment and I was able to tell him that I now preach about that. I preach about the environment and the need to be concerned about the Rain Forest, the air we breathe. Asthma is going out of control in the British Isles and this is linked with the environment. God is concerned about all these things and we can do something about them.

It is a shame that so many evangelical Christians not only have little concern for the environment, but are sometimes known as anti-environmental. How can this be when our Creator God has asked us to care for his creation? Pollution of the earth is totally unacceptable. But this is an issue that our young people care about, and if we don't connect with them on valid issues such as preservation of the environment. How then can we expect them to listen to us at all?

Why do so many people throw rubbish all over the place? Have you ever walked and seen all the rubbish? Sometimes my wife and I go for a walk and I take a bag and pick up rubbish as I go. Little things count with God! The Bible says if you give someone a glass of water you will get a reward. Are you out of the box enough to think that picking up a discarded bottle/can that could hurt someone, a child as they could cut or injure themselves, might get you some kind of reward? Hey, are you willing to think out of the box? Do you know what that means, those of you who are older? Out of the box is a young expression. It means that you are not just conforming to the same old ways; it means that you are willing to be different. Brothers and Sisters, let us start thinking about the environment, because that is also going to enable us to talk to many young people who have made this a big thing, maybe they have made this too big of a thing. If they don't know Jesus and are only concerned about animals and the environment then they are making a big mistake as they will never get to heaven through doing these good works. But by talking and listening to them, sympathizing where you can, you may see them come to know Jesus. It is so worth reaching out of your own comfort zone even to people who do not understand. I am a pilgrim; I am a struggler. I fail and I constantly have to crawl back to the cross and re-read books like *Calvary Road* and be filled afresh with the Holy Spirit.

7. The Lukewarm Christian

It has been many years since I started to share on the 7 Global Scourges and eventually I based the message on the story of the Good Samaritan in Luke 10. I started to add "lukewarmness" about which I have been preaching for 53 years in a different message. In some messages Number 6 is "The Unborn" and Number 7 is "The Environment." These are listed on the back of my business card that I distribute and this is the list on my website; www.georgeverwer.com. (I hope you can take a look at it!)

I have always believed that abortion is wrong. Mrs Payne, who was in OM spoke on this 30 years ago. I went on a Pro-Life March back in the eighties in Omaha, Nebraska with a local church. When my good friend Dr. Francis Schaeffer went into this in a major way towards the end of his life, I wondered about this, especially as I was living outside the USA, where people generally are more liberal in their thinking and often react to what they feel is "American pro-life extremism." I made a big mistake in my failure to speak out about abortion and I thank the Lord that a few years ago after reading, praying and seeing our whole Movement become more holistic that I took the step to become more pro-active in this important area. Abortion is a horrendous thing. Have you seen photos of a fetus after a few weeks? No one has the right to take the life of that little child. I highly esteem women and I know that there are very complex situations at times, but they do not have the right to take a life. Most men and women of God are in agreement on this, yet, often we are silent.

I then linked up with Randy Alcorn who has helped us flood his book, *Why Pro-Life* around the world. We are helping to translate this into languages, some of whom almost have nothing on this subject. I would be happy to send it free to anyone who asks for it. This book is very down-to-earth and does not just hit people with Scripture verses as that doesn't always mean much to those who are not believers. I would urge every one of you to become more committed and active in this area of challenge and that you will be able to read this book.

However, it is true that lukewarmness among the Lord's people is probably the greatest single global crisis in the Body of Christ. It is not an either–or situation, but both. So, the seventh person lying by the side of the road is the lukewarm Christian. I believe that lukewarmness in the church is greater than all of the other problems.

There is a danger in thinking that somehow all the problems are out there. In reality, often the problems are here. Lukewarmness is a scourge. I had been in meetings where a high percentage of people in the meeting acknowledged that they were lukewarm. They stood up to repent, ask for forgiveness and pray the verses in Acts 4:31 "to go forth and speak the Word of the Holy Spirit" with boldness.

Don't confuse basic lukewarmness with battling with lukewarmness. We all at times battle lukewarmness. I have to battle lukewarmness just as I have to battle with wrong attitudes and impatience. Don't succumb, and give in. Don't stop studying the Bible because it is boring. Perhaps the one exception to this is the person suffering from chronic medical depression, a very unique kind of illness. Those people need unique, special attention, concern, and prayer, but most of us are not in that category. For most of us that is not our struggle. If it is, may you get the care that you need. It is not an easy road and many godly people have gone through that. My own wife went through depression for a year and by his mercy she came out of it. I am talking more about spiritual depression. This is about basic lukewarmness linked with neglecting the Word, prayer, getting discouraged or allowing bitterness to come in.

My wife and I have had many disappointments in our lives, but we know that disappointment can be God's appointment to do better things for his kingdom. Many of the things that keep us from lukewarmness are not necessarily positive things. Negative things can really keep us on our toes. So we learn from our pilgrimage how to respond to the environment and circumstances. Until we keep our spiritual temperature at a place, where it is not dependent on the weather, spiritually-speaking, we will never be God's marathon runners. Spiritually the weather does change, doesn't it? For us as God's people to mainly think about ourselves or even our own family and not reach out to the lonely, confused and bereaved is a great mistake and a breach of the teaching of Luke 10.

May God enable us to receive his Word. May he keep us from feeling totally overwhelmed and enable us to understand that even the smallest thing we do for any of these people lying by the road side will be honored in the kingdom. Many of you have already been doing this for years and pouring funds into global missions. May God bless you.

The new ship, Logos Hope will be more involved in the HIV/AIDS crisis, global poverty and in proclaiming this message that I have shared. Can you imagine the multiplication impact through prayer as we share these concerns? I don't remember who said, "It is easier to cool down a fanatic than to wake up a corpse." So let's not worry about becoming too enthusiastic for the global poor, too enthusiastic regarding HIV/AIDS, too enthusiastic concerning the problems of the environment. I don't think that too much enthusiasm is going to be our biggest problem. Let's take God's Word with all of our struggles, weaknesses and vulnerability; let's respond, making sure we are filled with the Holy Spirit. Let's not let lukewarmness get a hold of some areas of our lives so that we in turn can minister to all these groups of people we have spoken about.

A new generation of young people is here. Instead of condemning them, because they would rather play a video game than hear a boring sermon in the local church, we should try to understand video games and the huge impact that they have both for good and evil on our culture. This generation of children generally are more interactive. They don't just only want to listen, they want to get involved in the action. If they would be saved, they could be the generation that finishes the task of world evangelism, because they are willing to roll up their sleeves and get involved. As I meet young people, I tell you, God is working in this post-modern generation. Do not become one more old-age wet blanket just because they don't want to sing the same hymns that you were singing when you went to Sunday school in 1908 or whenever it was.

Let us pray: Our God and Father you have brought this Word to my heart. I have shared it and I cannot run away from it even though (maybe) I have tried. Lord, I believe that you are going to raise up those who will pray more concerning all these things, those who will help release more finance, those who will help release more workers. Lord, we pray of the harvest as we are taught in Luke and Matthew to send forth workers into the harvest field.

Chapter 10

A Wretch Like Me

Yes, sin is serious and incessant, but you don't have to live in defeat.

Once when I told my story at a mission's conference, a woman informed me I had a demon. Another time, I told my story at the huge Urbana Convention in 1987, and shortly afterward one of our mission ships the Logos sank. Someone called me over the phone and said that this was the judgment of God on me. (Actually, we were thinking to replace the ship; no one was hurt when it sank, and we thought of it as a blessing from God.) Some people have a strange view of God.

Most people don't want to hear Christian leaders admit their sins or say they still, on occasion, sin. Hardly any one wants to hear a leader say he's come to terms with his sinful nature. But I have. And I say so publicly. I wouldn't call my temptation by pornography, an addiction. My exposure to it has been infrequent. I don't look at it online. I won't pay for it. And I haven't had regular access to the magazines since I was a teenager. The temptation may be less, but does not go away even when we are older.

A neighbor told me that she prayed for me for two years, and at a Billy Graham crusade at age 16, I had a powerful conversion experience. After that, I knew that the pornography had to go, and so I burned my few magazines. If it were not for my conversion, pornography could have become a terrible addiction and would have led to immorality. Still, through most of my adulthood, I was subject to awful temptations and sometimes fell.

Over the years, I can honestly say, I haven't gone looking for pornography. It comes to me. And it takes me by surprise. One time while travelling to a strategic meeting in Edinburgh, Scotland, I found a magazine left in the lavatory. That happened again when I was aboard a ferry en route to Scandinavia.

A defining moment for me occurred more than 30 years ago as I was walking in the woods outside London. From a distance I saw something hanging in the branches of a tree. It was a pornographic magazine, shot through with bullet holes. Someone had hung it there for target practice. Satan targeted me! I wish I could say I destroyed that magazine and got the victory, but the truth is, in the woods that day, that magazine made a fool out of me.

I was in the woods for quite a while after my lustful episode before I could crawl my way back to the cross and ask for forgiveness. Most of the time since then, I have been able to withstand Satan's temptations. I wish I could say that was true every time, but I'd be lying. And in the woods, I found a new approach for my own sinfulness: when I sin I ask forgiveness, time after time.

Victorious Living

What's victorious living for the sinner? The absence of sin? The defeat of Satan at every temptation? Going undefeated for a whole season? If that's the measure, then I fail. And, I suspect, we all fail, and we will continue to fail without relief.

In my own life, giving myself the benefit of the doubt, I estimate I successfully resist temptation 95 percent of the time. But with the number of temptations we face, that's still a lot of failure!

Over the course of my 45 years as a Christian, I have failed, not only in the area of lust. There are far worse sins than sexual failure with a magazine. In my own life, irritability and anger are greater issues. For others, it's arrogance, or condemnation, or legalism. Victorious living, given our sinful nature, is not the absence of sin, but knowing what to do when we sin. 1 John 2:1 says, "Sin not." It is John's desire that Jesus, followers will not sin. *But if anybody does sin, we have one who speaks to the Father in our defence—Jesus Christ the Righteous One.*

When I sin, I am readily quick to confess. And when I confess, I undercut Satan's power. Satan is the deceiver, the adversary who wants me to believe lies (either I really haven't done anything wrong or I've sinned so horribly that I'm disqualified to serve the Lord). By honest confession, my strength to battle the next temptation is bolstered by the knowledge that the Evil One has nothing with which to condemn me. Christ is my defender before the Father, and Christ says I am forgiven. Satan has nothing to say.

Since the moment of my salvation, I have never doubted God's Word about his love for me. It is vital that we realize God loves us and accepts us—even when we fail. That has been life-sustaining for me. Even when rejected by people for my sins, or for telling about my sins, I have always felt God's love. I have an open invitation to return to him as soon as I am ready to admit that sin once again has gotten the better of me.

God's love is not a license to sin. Grace without discipline can lead to disgrace. While God can forgive my disgraces, for the Christian leader, too many disgraces are not credible. People's ability as a leader will be gone. Paul said, *I beat my body and make it my slave so that after I have preached to others, I myself will not be disqualified for the prize* (1 Cor. 9:27). If I had not dealt with my habit quickly and kept it in a small arena of my life, my sin would have grown towards the point that I would be disqualified. It is only through the power of Christ that I am able to bring myself under subjection.

I have made myself accountable to my wife in the area of lust, and she has been an enormous source of affirmation for me. She prays for me. She listens to me. I report my occasional struggle to her and she does not condemn me. I remember telling her, now as an older man, that a quick glimpse at pornography had caused quite a stir in me physically. "Well", she said, "at least it proves you've got something left." I can be honest with my wife, and she with me.

A Sinner Mentoring Sinners

I have tried to be affirming for those who seek from me an accountability relationship. As creatures bent to sinning, we cannot master our sins alone. We need others who accept our sinfulness, but who will keep us from surrendering to it.

My special "mentoring" ministry began with my own public confession. I was invited to speak to the Urbana Missions Conference in 1967. My message was not about missions. It was my testimony and a general challenge to radical commitment. It included honesty about lust. That was the first time I gave my testimony in a large setting. Some were upset that I spoke so bluntly, but I told those young people that they, like me, needed to repent of sexual immorality. Some 4,000 stood up at the invitation, many weeping with repentance.

I have spoken at Urbana three times since then, and every time, I am inundated with people who need someone who will hear their struggle without condemning them, and point them again to

Christ. One young man wrote to me from the mission field. He asked me to meet him at the border of the country where he was stationed as he was grieving over his sin. He couldn't even verbalize it, so he typed out a page describing his addictions. I took him on as a helper/partner for one year (I've always had students traveling with me). This gave us the time to work through his problems. Later he returned to the mission field, and today he has a wonderful wife and family. He needed someone who would tell him, from experience, that there's hope.

Too often the church gives false ideas regarding holiness. We all want to mature in holiness, but it takes time. Growth comes with age and experience. Legalistic principles aren't the answer to the human sin mystery. I urged him to seek the balance between grace and discipline and encouraged him to read more widely. Books about the heroes of faith must be leavened with honest appraisals of their failings. Even the greatest among us are as much sinners as saints. We must set before ourselves realistic examples of those who have pursued holy standards and, in our halting two-steps forward, one-step-back fashion, get near them.

Leaders who admit their vulnerabilities, and even their failures, walk with a limp. But I suppose that's what makes it possible for hurting people to catch up with us to ask for help.

God's Service Is Handicapped Accessible

Despite my limp, God still uses me in his service. (This is part of the mystery of grace for me.)

As a very young Christian, I was in Indianapolis passing out tracts just outside a strip tease show. The show's billboard caught my eye, and soon I was seated in the third row watching the show. Within a few minutes, a rush of emotion hit me. I realized where I was, the evangelist, his pockets stuffed with tracts, was ogling young women as they took off their clothes one piece at a time. I ran from the club to the bus station nearby and into a phone booth. I picked up the phone and I called out to God. "Oh, God!" I pleaded. "Forgive me, forgive me."

I didn't feel forgiven, but I knew his promise to forgive us if we ask. Some minutes later, I told myself, "I am forgiven. Thank you, Lord," and I left the phone booth. But after the forgiveness comes the condemnation. "God can't use you. You've failed him," the Accuser said. Before I could say anything, a man walked up to me. I expected him to ask for the time or directions to the bus, but he started telling me his troubles. In a few minutes, he asked, "How can I be saved?" Within an hour, we knelt by the War Memorial in Indianapolis, and he surrendered his life to Jesus Christ.

I couldn't make up such a good story. Satan wanted me in the strip club, going deeper and deeper into the degradation of lust and pornography. His back-up plan would have me wallowing in the anguish of the phone booth for the rest of my life. But by God's grace, my repentance and receiving forgiveness by faith, I got back to God's plan, and he used me to lead this man to salvation. If ever I needed evidence of forgiveness and restoration, I had it.

I'm a sinner, who's growing stronger through the years, who crawls back to the cross when he sins and finds God still loves him and will still use him to bring others to Christ. That's grace, isn't it.

Chapter 11

Ten Challenges in Missions
(Counting the Cost)

Jesus said,

> "Suppose one of you wants to build a tower. Will he not first sit down and estimate the cost to see if he has enough money to complete it? For if he lays the foundation and is not able to finish it, everyone who sees it will ridicule him, saying, 'This fellow began to build and was not able to finish.'
>
> "Or suppose a king is about to go to war against another king. Will he not first sit down and consider whether he is able with ten thousand men to oppose the one coming against him with twenty thousand? If he is not able, he will send a delegation while the other is still a long way off and will ask for terms of peace. In the same way, any of you who does not give up everything he has cannot be my disciple.
>
> "Salt is good, but if it loses its saltiness, how can it be made salty again? It is fit neither for the soil nor for the manure pile; it is thrown out. 'He who has ears to hear, let him hear.'" (Luke 14:28–35, NIV)

Knowing the Situation

At the beginning of a consultation such as this, it is appropriate to count the cost. It is important when we are in a spiritual conflict to know what our situation really is. The Bible teaches about spiritual warfare.

The church situation today in Britain is very badly divided. A leader of one of the great evangelistic thrusts going on in this country, has written an article indicating, "We are not ready to evangelize."

My heart pounds in agreement with a lot that he states. There are great tensions and divisions in the British Church. I am convinced, however, that considering the claims of Christ, we cannot wait until all the church is united, until all gossip ceases and everybody is loving one another. This is because we have a commission and an example in the Book of Acts that evangelism goes forward even in the midst of weakness. Though the church in some ways maybe weak, God is greater. Evangelism, not just nationwide, but world evangelism must go forward. It must go forward as we also emphasize revival, holiness, spiritual life, and simultaneously declare war against all gossip, unbelief, sin, all that divides true believers.

There is no reason why we cannot simultaneously work toward renewal, revival, and world evangelism. I can share honestly with you that my first burden is not world evangelization, but the glory of God. One of the reasons that we in Operation Mobilisation have been able to place people in the Muslim world and keep them there for five, or ten, or even fifteen years, is because as we went there our first burden was not the conversion of Muslims, or the establishing of the church in the Muslim world, but the glory of God. Many of God's people, I believe, have missed his perfect will. I am not convinced that it is the will of God for all these People Groups to have no witness. We cannot take some extreme Calvinistic cop out and blame it all on God any more than William Carey, who could do that when they told him so many years ago, "If God wants the heathen to be reached, then he will take care of it, without the likes of you." It is God's plan because it's revealed in his Word that these people hear the gospel; that they receive a witness. It's impossible for us to predict how much fruit there will be. Our first burden is the glory of God, therefore, we obey him and we go forth to lay down our lives in witness.

Renewal

My second greatest burden is for renewal among God's people. When I say that, I'm not referring to any one stream. I'm happy to see people renewed in any way the living God chooses to do it. The way it happens in California isn't the way it happens in Sweden, and the way it happens in Sweden is not necessarily the way it happens in Germany. God does not destroy our humanity nor our nationality when he works in us. Only as we understand different cultures are we going to be able to see more recruits coming from these cultures. Of course, then they will have the job of trying to understand the cultures they go to. In speaking about the Holy Spirit and the victorious life, Billy Graham said, "I don't care how you get it, just get it." I long to see a combination of emphases on holiness, godly living, commitment, discipleship, the simple lifestyle and spiritual revolution; and to see them combined with outreach to every nation, and every people in world evangelism and cross-cultural communication. Count the cost. We know the words of the Lord Jesus in Matthew 9:37, *The harvest truly is plenteous, but the labourers are few.*

This is a very serious and needed consultation. I can objectively say that because I had nothing to do with the organization. I know the criticism that goes on against consultations and congresses. For people that are widely read, it sounds like a lot is taking place, but the average person may not be that widely read. Most of you were not invited to Thailand, or Lausanne, or wherever such meetings are going on. But somehow you have managed even as feeble, weak students to squeak in the door of this consultation. Such a consultation is needed because the situation is desperate. All kinds of consultations are taking place right now to try to solve the Iraq–Iran crisis. Endless money will be spent. They know that the crisis in the Middle East could bring on World War III. Beloved, as followers of Jesus Christ we are already in a warfare that makes the Iran–Iraq crisis look small, at least spiritually speaking.

Therefore, to have a consultation concerned about half of the people of the world, the unreached people, to pray, work and plan together and do anything we possibly can to increase the thrust, our numbers, and our unity, is well worth it.

Building Together

It's very easy to criticize. There is far too much criticism among evangelicals today, and far too many negative thinkers. In Philippians we're challenged to think on that which is good, pure and right. Anybody can tear down, but it takes an architect to build. May God make each one of you a spiritual architect to build for God as Nehemiah was sent forth by God, built despite opposition, mocking, and a lack of resources. We are called to build together.

There is a verse in Nehemiah that often challenges me when I may be doing something, I don't like to do. (You will never be a missionary if you don't like to do some things you have to do.) This verse speaks about having a mind to work. Would you pray with me that God will give us a mind to work?

Commitment

We're committed to Christ, to his Word and to world evangelism. But do we really know what that word means? It seems to me that in many countries and in cultures, especially in affluent societies, this word is losing its meaning. People talk about total commitment and then drive away in their new car to live in their million dollar home; and no one can say anything lest you be accused of being embarrassing or something worse.

In a world where millions are starving, where tens of millions have no homes, where evangelists in India are praying that they might have a bicycle (and some have been praying for ten years), those of us from the affluent section, I believe, have sinned against God, and therefore, have failed to understand Christ's demands upon our lives. Luke 14:33 is very clear: *Likewise, whosoever he be of you that forsaketh not all that he hath, he cannot be my disciple.* If there is going to be a powerful missionary invasion in our day, there must be a return to the standard of Jesus Christ and of the New Testament. An abomination that some of our countries are now propagating—a doctrine that teaches all spiritual people will prosper financially, has confused thousands. When people get into that doctrine, it doesn't work, they go away feeling that they are unspiritual or that they are not men and women of faith.

A. W. Tozer said that the more keen Christian is easily led astray. The more keen (enthusiastic, excited, boldly dedicated) Christian, is more easily led astray. When I first started preaching about world missions twenty-five years ago, the main message was world missions, total commitment and all that side of the challenge which is in the Word of God. As I went on and saw the strategy of the enemy, I had to start speaking about extremism, calling people to spiritual balance, and to compare Scripture. One of the greatest hindrances to world evangelism and to the vision that you and I have is extremism. My whole life is involved with students and young people. The amount of extremism in Europe among students is just unbelievable. There are little house groups that don't believe in world missions. I've heard tapes, more or less explaining that world missions is a thing of the past.

Unlimited Possibilities

As we count the cost, seeing "the fields that are ripe unto harvest," there are unlimited possibilities for short-term evangelistic opportunities. Isn't it amazing that the Mormons have 20 to 30 thousand men on the field? They have over 100,000 converts in Britain alone. They want to have some 70 or 80 thousand men on the field by the turn of the century. The church of Jesus Christ should have at least, at any one time (apart from the standard missionary force) 100 thousand men on a one or two year program. I recently read something countering the concept that we needed a great number of missionaries, that there were so many of us that we would start to get in the way. I wonder if they have ever visited a country like Italy? When I went to Italy, the student work there consisted of two middle-aged ladies trying to reach all the university students in Italy. It has not improved very much since.

The challenge of world evangelism is as great as ever. These huge numbers of missionaries that are being prayed for, can be used if they are Spirit-controlled and committed people. I don't think that they will get in the way of each other and hinder the national church if they know a few of the basic rules—like submitting to the national leadership in that country, working alongside people, not lording it over them, but learning from them and turning the leadership to nationals as quickly as possible. Let us count the cost and realize that we are in a spiritual warfare. Satan has a strategy and he will counter-attack. He has many dead-end streets into which he likes to get God's people.

Committed to Each Other

We need to count the cost in terms of our commitment to one another. How easy it is today for each group and each individual and to some degree, even churches to do their own thing. This has so overwhelmed me at times that I have wanted to leave my own fellowship simply, so that I could be identified with the whole body. We need one another, different fellowships, different organizations. And we have different ideas and will never all agree on every point, but if we are going to evangelize the world, we are going to have to build up our relationships.

This is another reason why such consultations are to be valued. We get to know one another and understand what others are doing. I attended a mini-seminar at the World Congress on Evangelism in Lausanne and found that a great experience. It was a humbling experience to attend this Congress as in OM I'm the leader. People are very kind to me and I am esteemed. I walk into a place and they let me say a few words. But when I arrived at the World Congress on Evangelism I was just one of a thousand, a nobody with all these great men of God, such as Dr. Schaeffer and John Stott; you are just humbled.

When you get together with God's people and hear about their work and all that God is doing around the world, I tell you that is a good therapy. You realize that little OM, with all its ships and whatever else is just a drop in the ocean. What a great experience for our spiritual growth to be brought into a situation where we are just part of the body! You know that when you are in that situation, your joy will have to come from the Lord himself. There is always the danger when we come together, we try to get bits of joy from one another. The Word of God tells us "not to be ministered unto but to minister." We are going to have to look to the Lord, or we will be overwhelmed by the challenge or by so many interesting people. I'm convinced that God wants us to build our relationships.

In OM we have been trying more in our nights and days of prayer to pray for other missions, fellowships, and groups. We bring in visiting speakers, look at their slides, find out what they are doing, and God has blessed us as we have done that. Many people in their own country do not know what other groups are doing even in a peripheral way. I do not know whether they don't read Christian magazines or they don't like people. One fellow said, "Not that I am anti-social, I just don't like people." It is valuable to know what others are doing because then we know something of what God is doing. We should rejoice with those who rejoice. God helps us if we rejoice when our work has a victory. We rejoice when any member of the Body of Christ is being used or blessed. We attempt as the Scriptures teach us to believe the best about other fellowships and about other groups.

Being Strong-Minded

When you get into missionary work, you are going to discover that you are involved with a wide range of strong-minded people. A lot of the missionaries in the world are such people. That's how they got first place. Very few of you are ever going to get to the mission field unless you dig your heels in, a bit. Auntie isn't wanting you to go, or maybe Mummy and Daddy aren't either. Your own pastor may not even want you to go, or your employer, because the teaching in England now is, go to university, get a good job, make money, then when you are settled, if the Lord leads, go to the mission field.

I want to know, how many have gone to the mission fields through that kind of philosophy? Once people are married and settled down, generally they are stuck for life. Very few married couples with children are launching out to the mission field, apart from those who already started to move before they got into that more interesting, complicated and frustrating phase of life. I believe the enemy is very, very clever, and he has a massive propaganda machine. That machine is opposed to world missions. We need wisdom and discernment to know what is coming from the enemy and what is coming from the Lord. A.W. Tozer said, "The greatest gift needed in the church today is the gift of discernment," and we desperately need this.

Communicating Cross-Culturally

We have got to count the cost of building relationships. Do you get on with people? Do you know how to listen to people, how to let love cover differences when someone says something that you don't like? If you don't, you are going to have difficulties, not only in missionary work, but in your life too. I don't think that we can overemphasize the need to learn how to relate to people and to communicate cross-culturally.

Many of us have trouble communicating in our own culture. We must be very careful here that we don't get discouraged thinking about it. Someone wrote recently that, we can't really communicate cross-culturally unless we have the gift of cross-cultural evangelism. I haven't met many people who claim to have this gift, and it's obvious that people who read such books are not planning on going to the mission field. For 25 years I have seen simple humble people apply themselves in a foreign country as a servant, a learner, walking Calvary's road, and I have seen them effectively communicate cross-culturally, encourage and work with nationals and vice-versa.

I am convinced that each one of us, to some degree can communicate cross-culturally. Some of course will be more gifted, but each one of us can communicate. There are a lot of things that we have to learn and books that we can read like *Share Your Faith with a Muslim* etc. One out of every six people in the world is a Muslim. Less than two percent of the missionaries in the world work among Muslims. Are we going to wait for those who feel that they have to have a special Muslim cross-cultural gift? We have enough obstacles to get over to get people to the field, much less putting up new ones! It is my sincere prayer that we will beware of this kind of thinking.

The idea that we need more and more studies so that we can do our job better is very much linked with intellectualism. It is text-book theory. But be out on the field for ten, or twenty, or at least two years and you will see that it is just not true. Think of the great movement of the Assemblies under the leadership of Bakht Singh in India, a movement I'm personally familiar with. Ordinary men, many of them without much education, filled with the Word of God, started churches and communicated cross-culturally. Many Muslims have come to Jesus Christ, and 300 Assemblies exist today.

A Destructive Enemy

Lately I've read of a number of Christian organizations that are going through tremendous times of difficulty and disunity.

The warfare is real. As we have seen some great Christian personalities in America hit the divorce courts, our hearts have sunk, and we have been reminded that it is not a game, or some kind of a religious carnival. It is all out warfare, in which the enemy is out to destroy people. When you enroll in the army of God and decide to reach out to the unreached and be involved in God's great purpose of world evangelization you will be a marked person. If you don't know how to pray, to resist Satan, if you don't have a disciplined life, and know how to share and fellowship in a way that is going to help you; if you don't know how to wear the armor of God, and hold high the shield of faith, wherewith you can stop all the fiery darts of the devil, then you will be one more missionary casualty.

Quality, not Quantity

My greatest concern (it may sound like a contradiction) is not firstly more missionaries; it is the quality of the missionary that we train and send out, that is all-important. We have to count the cost of what it takes to gain quality of life—not perfection, nor super-spirituality, nor the total supernatural disciplined person (a sort of bionic evangelical), but rather quality of life in reality, brokenness, openness, and all that we can appropriate in Jesus Christ, for we are complete in him. A.W. Tozer was a great missionary thinker, and very much involved in world missions. He said that the task of the church is twofold:

to spread the gospel throughout the world and to make sure that the Christian faith she spreads is a pure New Testament kind. The church will always produce itself after its kind. A worldly-minded, unspiritual church is sure to bring forth on her shores, a Christian faith much like her own. Not only the naked Word, but the character of the witness determines the quality of the convert. He goes on to say that the popular notion, that the first obligation of the church is to spread the gospel to the outermost parts of the earth, is false. Her first obligation is to be spiritually worthy to spread it—to spread a degenerate brand of Christian faith to non-Christian lands is not to fulfill the commandment of Jesus Christ.

Tozer's statement has meant a great deal to me. It would be a glorious thing if many of us here would renew our commitment first to the Lord Jesus Christ himself and to wherever he leads us. The last thing we would want a consultation like this to produce is a lot of people with a guilt complex if somehow they don't quite make it to the Muslim world. God is wanting to deal with you and me on the basis of love, grace, and mercy. What happens is that people may go out to serve just long enough to get rid of their guilt trip and then they come home. I'm convinced that some of you who are afraid of missionary work have these ideas of cockroach invasions, eating all kinds of weird food and suffering in extreme climates. If you would understand God's ways and move by faith, many of you would discover that you actually enjoy it when you get to those countries. The true missionary is not some kind of ascetic who is perpetually pining for the California beaches and MacDonald hamburgers. (In any case, MacDonalds are getting there faster than we are!) I have seen on the mission field, in Spain, Belgium, Holland and then India, that in the midst of the battle there are many wonderful and enjoyable aspects of missionary life. It is one of the fullest and most challenging occupations anyone could ever get into. Of course, we are all missionaries, but I'm talking about when you move out of your own culture.

The Call

Let's count the cost, what it's going to take in terms of quality of life. Then let's have a plan over the next couple of years to build up our spiritual lives through the Word, prayer, fellowship, the cross, feeding on some of the powerful Christian books and great ministry that we can get on tape and CDs. The Word of God says: "I commend you to his Word, the Word of his grace which is able to build you up and give you an inheritance among them who are sanctified" (Acts. 20:32).

God may give you a crisis experience during this week which may be a turning point in your life. God is working in different people in different ways. Some people have very emotional missionary calls. They can tell you the moment and the hour. Johnny Jungle came back from New Guinea, and was showing slides in the church, and at that moment you were hit, "Lord, take me; I'll go." I've heard some of the most unbelievable stories of how people were called to the mission field. Praise the Lord! As long as you go, and persevere, the Lord uses you, it's fine.

Many of you are never going to get that kind of emotional call, so stop looking for it. If somehow you feel you must have it, let me know, and I will send one of my coworkers, and at midnight we will show some slides, play some music in your room, and the next morning you will be ready to go. I can assure you that you probably will not get very far! Some of the people who are doing the greatest work on the mission field are laid back people with far less emotion, who perhaps never had a special call, but slowly it was revealed to them by the Lord guiding them, others instructing, or giving advice that this was the way, and they walked in it. Sometimes messages on the will of God leave us all the more confused than when we started, because it's a narrow message and gives a narrow way to following

God's will. As well as working in different people in different ways, God is working in different groups in different ways. He is working through the Navigators, Campus Crusade, and others who perhaps don't feel they should fellowship that much with other groups.

Right Priorities

When we think of the size of the task, it is vitally important to count the cost about the quality of our lives. Many of us have too many convictions. We must have discernment and wisdom to know what the priorities are! The "good" is enemy of the "best." Some people are caught up endlessly in secondary issues. That's all right, if you feel that way, but let's unite on the major issues of God's Word.

Even important biblical convictions, if they are not mixed with love, can turn to bitterness. If we're not careful, what we receive here eventually could turn to bitterness. I found this is possible as I have been preaching the message about the Muslim world for 24 years in many nations. Considering the amount of people that have heard the challenge, the response has been small. In trying to reach out to these countries, it seems so often that most of the churches are not with us. Often you are a lonely voice, crying out in the wilderness, and if you're not careful, you can become bitter, and God doesn't want bitter missionaries.

Probably most of us have heard of somebody returning from the field who suffered, and maybe was living on the barest essentials, and they saw the way people were living in their home country. When they started to speak in meetings, you could sense there was bitterness and harshness. It was not the sweetness of Jesus Christ. I feel, no matter how many times we are walked on, our message is thrown to one side; no matter how few people respond to our challenge, we must always remain loving, kind, tender and compassionate. We have no axe to grind; we only have a Savior to serve.

We must be patient in spreading this unique vision that we have for all the people of the world. I may have a few strong points, but I also have many weak points. I find far greater interest on the part of youth to move out in evangelism than I do in the church to send them out. That is not a statement against the church because there are many good churches that want to send out missionaries.

God has brought us to Edinburgh for a great purpose. Those of us especially in this Student Consultation are not the most famous, strongest or the most educated, but if Jesus Christ be for us, who can be against us? Let us stand together, uniting the great qualities of spiritual reality with the great vision of reaching all people with the gospel and believe by faith that it can come to pass. The decision is always ours. God will take us so far, lovingly pushing and drawing us, but the ultimate step to be a doer instead of just a hearer is always yours.

I hope you will take it.

Note: As you read this chapter, keep in mind this message was given many years ago at a Student Consultation in Edinburgh organized by Ralph Winter.

Chapter 12

Some Very Basic Truths

1. Prayer

The bottom-line in the mobilization of new workers must be prayer. Matthew 9:35 is very clear on this point, as is Acts 13:1–5. More prayer for our existing workers and all those in the training process is equally important. We urgently need more prayer gatherings of all kinds.

2. Attitude

God is concerned about our attitude—attitude towards him and towards others. The second commandment is to love our neighbors as we love ourselves.

I am concerned about our attitude towards other Christian leaders, especially those who may not agree with us. Sometimes even when mentioning someone's name, you can see a wrong attitude on a person's face or in his words.

3. Repentance

Surely, together with prayer, the reality of the cross and the Holy

Spirit is the key to personal revival. We are trying to flood across the world, Roy Hession's book, *The Calvary Road*, because for over 40 years God has been using this powerful message to bring people into humility, real brokenness and then a life of love and faith.

4. Disciples

In our ministry, God wants to give us disciples—true converts to Christ who go on for him in growth and all the aspects of the Christian life. We must not be deceived into thinking that all those who make some kind of decision are now "saved" and are true believers. Praise God some are, and time will tell this. Praise God for every church, and every small group or mentoring program where people are being discipled. Praise God for the Navigators and others who have been such a great example.

5. Discipline

Without this there will be few real disciples. I fear that some messages about deliverance and the Holy Spirit give people the idea that discipline is not something spiritual. What are we going to do with the clear command of Jesus to deny self, take up the cross daily and follow him? What about Paul's words concerning buffeting his body and bringing it into subjection? Jesus said, "If you love me, keep my commandments." We must model and teach the disciplined life to all our new recruits even if they are coming for a summer. To fail to do so is to make a tragic mistake.

6. Courage

In these days of terrorism, unrest and the persecution of God's people, we need great courage. I see it as one of the greatest needs in my life right now. If you are in leadership, you will especially need more courage, which of course, is linked with faith and deep trust in

God and his Word. The way ahead will not be easy and all the fiery darts of hell will come our way as we go forward.

7. Wisdom

Maybe a better word is discernment. A.W.Tozer said it was the greatest need in the church. When selling books and Bibles in my hometown as a young Christian I met a lady who challenged me to read the Proverbs every day. There is one for every day in a month. She said, "A Proverb a day keeps the devil away." I have been reading them almost every day ever since. It has been a huge blessing and help.

In my own books I have tried to pass on some of the wisdom God has given me from his Word and through other people.

Chapter 13

Keeping the Balance
Reality–Grace–Action

We have tried to emphasize balance, but in many areas of life we have not found it easy. One of my own greatest struggles is between grace and discipline. For any of you who think this is not a problem, I would say you probably have not looked at issues and realities.

We need to have certain basic laws and rules just to function. Non-Christians know this and are creating more rules and laws by the day. Where I live, you can be fined £50 if your dog fouls the sidewalk. When I walk my daughter's dog I carry a little plastic bag; am I a legalist?

The truth is that no matter how "grace awakened" and "bighearted" we are, we still must learn to keep the basic rules of the game.

In the area of basic morality, we must make every effort in God's power to "keep the rules." We all know people who were killed due to, in some cases, one quick simple act of indiscipline. Many car accidents take place, because for a moment the driver lets his eyes or mind wander from the road. I really believe we need a "wake-up call" in this area before it is too late.

The fact is that no one can function, Christian or non-Christian, without basic rules and law-keeping discipline. We must work and think hard; we must organize our time and work; we must know the basic laws and rules of our country, city and job, and keep them. When we sin or fail, we can be forgiven, especially by God and often (not always) by people.

It's hard for me to admit, but sometimes we are reading too many books, especially of a certain kind, and we need to lay them aside for a while and come down to earth. In some cases, this is harder for the "spiritually-minded Christians" than for some non-Christians.

We must take full responsibility for our life and behavior. We must stop blaming God, our friends, the system or demons and spiritually speaking, "bite the bullet" of ordering and disciplining our lives. All sports people (read Hebrews 12) who are any good have disciplined their bodies and aimed and worked for excellency. All of us in God's marathon must do the same; no more excuses!

The balance is kept especially in how we respond when other people sin, fail and really blow it, maybe even causing great harm. As God's people, we must respond in grace and love. We must try to find a grace-awakened solution and keep a godly attitude in the midst of the problem or crisis. The person(s) may need to be disciplined.

In God's work we must have basic rules, and we must be mature enough to face the consequences when we break them. One of the confusing, hurtful statements that some people make is, "It's easier to get forgiveness than permission." To do something wrong to start with, wow! The devil has had a field day with that one. Remember, in certain secular situation you would be fired.

We have learned some lessons on our ships over the past 30 years. Partly because they knew we would forgive, people have walked down the gangway into serious sin. By the way, in one sense, every sin is serious. I had a letter from a person who did that some years ago, and said that his life has been a total chaotic mess ever since.

The truth is that life in itself can be very harsh and very hard. The sooner we learn that and stop making excuses, the better our progress. In voluntary Christian ministry, certain kinds of unreality are especially prevalent. We seem to more easily blame the agency, team or the leader. Their sins and shortcomings are a factor that makes it hard to know how to react. In some situations, there is no easy answer and seemingly win-win situation. Sometimes, it's only "damage control."

In our work, when we finally ask someone to leave, we often encounter great problems as the person being disciplined calls it "unfair" or even starts a gossip campaign against the leader or even the organization. Yes, welcome to God's work, planet earth.

We must continue to emphasize grace, and show people in every way that God loves them even when they sin or fail. Even if the person commits a crime, yes, even murder, they can be forgiven by God—but to get forgiveness from the legal system, judge or jury is going to be different. As we bring justice and judgment into the picture, the battle for balance becomes even more complex.

In our emphasis on love and forgiveness, in all our care and counseling about grace, love and acceptance, we must try to keep the big picture. Some Christians with their inexpensive advice can often make the whole event more complicated. We have found that, it is one thing to preach about God using the weak, needy, fallen ragamuffin, sometimes eccentric people (there are books about them), but quite something else to live with one on your team or even have one as your leader. Are we dealing with contradiction or paradox?

Yes, this is a huge challenge and we will never fully agree on the many aspects of it, but my prayer after you read this is for greater balance, reality and consistency on every level. Forgive me if I am aiming too high.

Chapter 14

Dangers of the Tongue

As I write this, my heart is very heavy. My hate for sin, Satan, and self is on the increase. I know that Satan is trying to destroy individuals. He doesn't attack ships, trucks, or church buildings, but rather he attacks people. I have ample proof that one of Satan's main methods which is being used in these days is the sins of the tongue. Even as I write this, I want to search my own heart, and I come in repentance for words that never should have come from my mouth.

Please read and meditate on these words. . .

> For, brethren, ye have been called unto liberty; only use not liberty for an occasion to the flesh, but by love serve one another. For all the law is fulfilled in one word, even in this; Thou shalt love thy neighbour as thyself. But if ye bite and devour one another, take heed that ye be not consumed one of another (Galatians 5:13–15).

I would urge all teams to make a prayerful study of the sins of the tongue. Please read and meditate on the following Proverbs:11:13; 12:19,22,25; 14:23; 15:1,4; 17:9,28; 18:19; 20:19. We all know many New Testament passages which bring out these truths. Have your team members look up some of these. Matthew 18:15–20 should also be studied and put into practice.

We hear there is an "OM grapevine." This could be the devil's telegraph system. For news to be passed from one to another is fine, unless it brings a brother or sister into a negative light. Philippians 4:8 should be our guide. Those of us who teach and preach will be even more guilty according to James 3:1.

Satan is clever— and some of us maybe doing things without being aware of it. See 2 Corinthians 2:11. We must be more prayerful and careful when we pass on any information about others.

Matthew 7:12 is another basic rule. Leaders at times must prayerfully evaluate and discuss people. This is why it seems to me that a person who gossips should be disqualified from leadership.

I am 100 percent convinced that some leaders have wrong impressions about other leaders that can be traced back to gossip which, I believe, includes insinuations. The latter is almost more deadly. If we are guilty, then let us repent and put things right.

Team members must be careful of what they say about their leader. God's Word says, *Against an elder receive not an accusation, but before two or three witnesses* (1 Timothy 5:19).

One of the most foolish things we can do is pass on to a brother or sister something negative and harmful which someone has said about them. Proverbs says this can separate the best of friends. We have seen this happen in the past. When tempted to do such an evil thing, remember the person who said it may have repented or changed his mind, and so what you pass on becomes a lie. Let us avoid such a practice, like the plague.

Ultimately, when we sin with the tongue, we harm ourselves. The judgment we give will often be the judgment we receive.

I pray that every husband and wife in the work will read and heed these things, because as married people we should be more mature. If we know people who have clearly sinned in these matters, then let God's love and mercy flow towards them. If it is against you, then you must practice Matthew 18:15–20. Don't fall into the same pit in your effort to help them get out. For some complicated situations, there are no easy answers. If such situations drive us into worry, fear, depression, or discouragement, then we only play into the devil's hands. The blood of Christ can cover and cleanse. Let us press on with our eyes upon him.

P.S. All of us who feel needy in this area should make an extra effort to study all related verses and books which deal with these problems. Often our sins of the tongue are symptomatic of deeper spiritual needs.

Chapter 15

---◄◇►---

25 Point Strategy for Victory over Lust

1. Focus on Jesus.
2. Walk daily in God's Word.
3. Repent on a moment-by-moment basis.
4. Worship daily.
5. Meditate and memorize key Scriptures.
6. Share daily with others.
7. Share with others and walk in the light.
8. Realize God's acceptance of yourself.
9. Exercise daily.
10. Maintain balanced eating habit.
11. Sleep well and have a nap when possible.
12. Be active.
13. Have specific goals and aims.
14. Pray daily and praise God.
15. Read good books and magazines.
16. Listen to praise music and other music.
17. Read the Bible daily and listen to ministry tapes.

18. Travel with one or more companions, and wife when possible.
19. Avoid being completely alone with the opposite gender.
20. Avoid vulnerable zones like news-stands or places that sell pornography.
21. Beware of hotel rooms and stay with God's people. If in a hotel, disconnect TV.
22. Grow in deep bonding with your wife (or husband) in the knowledge of the Word.
23. Delight in good regular sex life with wife (or husband).
24. Enjoy good and acceptable aspects of our world and culture like a good movie, concerts, walks in scenic places, nice meals, rollercoasters, etc.
25. Keep a balance of truth.

Chapter 16

Amateurism vs Professionalism

I recently had a letter in which the subject of amateurism vs professionalism in missions was mentioned. Different articles are being written on this subject and it is leading some people into confusion. We now have one more controversy to deal with, though it's not new. Often these problems come when people are trying to sell, or oversell, their special vision or program. In their effort to do this, they often put down other people or ministries without realizing it.

I deal with this in my book, *Out of the Comfort Zone*. I personally feel that the use of these two words and the way people use them are very confusing.

Someone said, "OM is perceived as one of the agencies that recruits and deploys amateurs." This I believe gives a very false picture. . .plus what do they mean by the term amateurs? Are not the Olympics for amateurs?

Some groups, like OM, are both short and long-term with many people who would be called professionals, working alongside people with a wide variety of training and education. In our early days we had Cambridge and Oxford graduates who worked alongside people with very little formal education. Was one better than the other? All these people needed missionary orientation and training—some before they went on the field, and all of them on the field as well.

Where do we put Jesus and his disciples in all these? What about the two sent out in Acts 13? If we followed some people's line of thinking, then Jesus Christ and his twelve apostles were the ultimate amateurs! What about the ministry of the Holy Spirit?

Let's remember you can be trained and be a "professional" and still make huge blunders on the mission field, and of course, at home too. We tend to overreact to mistakes (I know I have sometimes) and quickly communicate that it would not have happened if the person had more training, teaching or better doctrine, etc. That can be an oversimplification, to say the least.

I am convinced that more time and effort we use to criticize one another (there is a place for criticism) should be used in reaching a lost world with the gospel.

We also need more research before we quickly go into print. The work of world missions has become highly complex, which is also true of the church in general. Unless we have a more balanced and grace-awakened approach towards one another and our different churches and movements, then I believe we are destined to greatly hinder what the Holy Spirit is trying to do across the world.

Satan has always tried to bring a wedge between those who have a strong emphasis on "on-the-job and field training" in comparison with academic training. Surely it is not either–or situation, but both. Some people are gifted in studying while out on the field, while others find this almost impossible and need the discipline that a good academic environment gives. I have a message called, "Why Go to Bible College?"

We have found that over the years, thousands who have come

short term, often for a specific purpose like working in the engine room on the ship, have later ended up in Bible college or something similar to further prepare for a different kind of ministry. Surely God leads different people in different ways, and he uses people in different ways. Greater obedience to Philippians 2:3 and 4 would bring a lot of balance and reality in all of these.

I submit this, as someone with much yet to learn.

Chapter 17

Encouraging Words for Those Who Have Served

Life After

I'm sitting in a train, heading back to my home in London after a church meeting in Bristol. I have been crying out to the Lord for the right words for this article, as I long to be able to help and encourage those who have been out on the mission field and are now home, or headed home.

Re-entry, as it is sometimes referred to, can be a greater challenge than going to the mission field in the first place! Seven challenging biblical words come to mind. I would like you to think about these words and allow them to remind you of great themes from God's Word.

Integrity

One of the greatest words in the English language is "integrity." It requires openness, honesty, purity and reality from us; it means we will not exaggerate what we have done or seen on the mission field; it means we will be especially careful about the sins of the tongue; and it means we must be absolutely honest and open in regard to finances.

Discipline

It has been proven thousands of times over, that *grace without discipline can equal disgrace.*

After a tough mission experience that demands hard work and discipline, it is easy to drop our guard in this area. Outside a team situation and leadership structure, we will have to shift gears into more of a self-discipline mode. In attempting to do this, it will be easy to mis-communicate and fail to find the balance. We might date a person who professes to be a Christian, yet wants to go to bed on the first date, or at least before marriage. Some people leave certain mission situations with a lot of pent-up sexual drive and when they get home to a loose and promiscuous environment, they easily let down their moral guard, ending up in a real mess.

Some folks quickly reject missionaries and don't want to keep contact, writing them off as super-spiritual or ascetic. Efforts to prove otherwise don't always succeed and feelings of rejection would easily come. Satan will do everything he can to discourage us; and when we are discouraged it opens the door to other temptations. We must daily hold high that shield of faith (Ephesians 6), or stop those fiery darts of discouragement.

Reality

I find that some people return from certain training programs and summer-mission events having a rather fantasy view of the Christian life. (This also can come in some churches and from reading certain kinds of books.) We must realize that no matter how filled we are with the Holy Spirit, we are still very much human. If we are realistic, we know that very good people—even committed Christians—can and will say and do very wrong and sinful things.

Terrible things also happen to good people. We love the Psalms and sometimes read Proverbs, but we tend to forget that those two great books are preceded by the Book of Job.

Vision

We must battle hard to keep the vision that God has given us. We should become senders and mission-mobilizers—missionaries for missions—making every attempt to pass on to others in reality and humility, what God has taught us on the field. This will not be easy and there will be many setbacks and discouragements on the way.

Sometimes it will be just one person at a time that we will be able to love, influence and help on the road to become a world Christian. Try to make good use of tools, like books, cassettes and CDs that can help people grasp what it's all about.

We need to stay in touch with people in missions, especially those we have helped come to Christ. Try not to break promises—If you have told people that you will pray for them, then you must pray for them. Try to fellowship, even by phone if necessary, with like-minded people. Keep that mission fire burning in your heart.

Grace

I would urge you to read Charles Swindoll's book, *The Grace Awakening*. This book, together with the book, *Re-Entry*, by Peter Jordan, could be a major factor in helping you face—in the power of the Holy Spirit—the challenges and difficulties that you are sure to confront at home. These books will help you to be big-hearted when people ask silly questions—or worse, no questions at all.

This revolution of grace helps us to accept and forgive people who seem so selfish or visionless. We must learn to graciously agree to disagree. We need to learn how to be aware of the most subtle forms of pride, even missionary pride. It will also help us keep on forgiving ourselves when we fail or sin. Grace will keep us in the center of God's highway of holiness. I also urge you to read Philip Yancey's book, *What's So Amazing about Grace*.

Forgiveness

Have you really forgiven those who have hurt you on the mission field? What about yourself? Have you forgiven yourself for blunders, mistakes and sins that you have committed? If so, you are on a good road, because now you can forgive those who hurt you back home. Beware of unrealistic expectations, most of all in connection with your mission agency and home church.

If you were greeted at the airport and given a royal reception, then praise the Lord. If not, still praise the Lord. Let your first source of joy and satisfaction be the Lord himself. Let human love and help be the water that spills over the top of the glass—the icing on the cake.

Please beware of unrealistic—often biblical—expectations. You must learn to love and accept people back in your home culture, just as you accepted those new people in that foreign land in their culture. I believe we need a contextualized approach to going home just as much as we do in going out. We need to be extra grateful to those who have prayed for us and supported us. We must esteem the senders and realize that they have an equal part in this great mission's task.

Proactive

How easy it is, when under pressure, to become re-active! Reaction is generally negative—the hard blows from life and people seem to hit below the belt. Those hits are not fair! Let's remember, 1 Corinthians 15:58, *Therefore, my dear brothers, stand firm. Let nothing move you. Always give yourselves fully to the work of the Lord, because you know that your labor in the Lord is not in vain.*

Let's keep on keeping on, and try not to be critical or negative about the local church, particularly if they did not help or support you that well. Please try to listen and discern their situation and some of the struggles they experienced while you were away.

Remember Philippians 2:3, . . .*but in humility consider others better than yourselves.* It is easy to see the problems in your own nation, city or church, though it can be very intimidating. We need that same boldness we had when we stepped off the airplane in Turkey, India or wherever.

We should stay active in prayer and evangelism, seeking out those from the countries we worked in, who are now immigrants or students in our hometown. We need to affirm that the mission field is everywhere and keep up a mission's vision foundation.

Well, my train is about to arrive in London and I wrote this all by hand on a shaky train table. I hope my secretary can read it. Wow! I hope you have read it as well.

God Bless You!

Chapter 18

Now That I'm Home. . .

Practical considerations for Mission workers on furlough, as well as those returning permanently to their homes after short or long-term service.

Dear Brothers and Sisters,

Greetings in the precious and powerful name of Christ.

When individuals or families are able to take a break from work, it may be for a few months or even a year; this provides a beneficial period of change and rest, as well as an opportunity for ministry to believers at home.

What I want to most strongly emphasize is that when you return home, Satan will not give up his vicious attempts to destroy you and your ministry. In no way can you expect your time at home to be easier than your time out on the field or at the summer campaign. It is here, I think, that many people have made their most fatal mistake. It is one thing to take a break; it is quite another to allow the shield of faith to drop to the ground and thereby to open the way for a fiery dart from Satan.

What are some of the dangers that you will face at home?

1. Immorality

In a new environment—especially if your home country is part of a promiscuous society (and which society is not?)—you may suddenly find more intensive temptation in this area. Usually at home you will not be submitting to leadership in the way that you did in the mission field and this could also lead to greater temptation. Satan may try to cause you to think you can do something back home that no one would ever find out about. Although this may be true to some extent, our burden is to live for Christ and not for men (Col. 3:23). I don't believe there is any period in our lives in which we may slack off in the kind of discipline we need in order to stand against this kind of fiery dart.

2. Special Treatment

In some nations, returning missionaries are treated almost like war heroes and this can be very dangerous. People constantly giving us gifts create a feeling that we have suffered so much. They want to make up for what we have supposedly sacrificed in the "regions beyond." The returning missionary suddenly finds himself gaining weight and this can be detrimental to health in the long run. (This also does not help his testimony when he returns to the field, especially when it is a Two-Thirds World country.)

In other situations, the opposite can happen and no one seems to be interested in the missionary or his work at all. Self-pity and hurt can set in if he is not careful.

Far more serious than this, however, is the subtle tendency to compromise one's convictions in various ways in order to "get along better" with the believers back home. This is an area where we need to find spiritual balance. We do need to know how to receive things from people and be gracious. Although I do not have an easy answer,

I believe great discernment is necessary in each and every situation and we should at least be aware of the possible dangers involved.

In some cases, people have found it very difficult to return, especially to a hot Two-Thirds World country. Some actually live from one furlough to the next, always looking forward to those wonderful days back home, where they can take advantage of all the special treatment from God's people.

3. Generalization

When we visit our homeland for a short period of time, we may come away with an incomplete picture of life. People often help us, and because we receive our financial support from others or from our church, we are often able to share in the blessings of life at home. However, we rarely share the problems of daily life faced by those who live in that country year in and year out. (The picture would be rather different if you went home and took up a difficult job and made your own living for a year. This would also be very different from a so-called "year off" traveling around, taking a few meetings, living with other people and having basic needs supplied.) It is important when in your own country not to make generalizations about what life is like there.

4. Effect upon the Children

Endless discussion could take place about the effect upon children on returning to the home country, as a family. In some cases, the furlough inspires the children with such a love for their home country, that they are never able to settle back into the country in which their parents are working. Sometimes it seems necessary that children have one particular country with which to identify. In our own case, at least two of our children identify far more with the field in which we are working, Great Britain, than they do with the USA. Our situation, of course, is quite different from those people who are unable to stay in a particular country more than just a few years.

Sometimes, changing from one culture to another can perplex a child, especially when he is put into a school for just one year. (I'm not totally convinced that it is valuable to take children out of school in a particular country in which the parents are working, and then enroll them in a school in the home country for that time. I am not strongly against this, as I know that sometimes it is simply impossible to do anything else, especially when someone is convinced that he must have a year-long furlough.)

Ultimately, we are cast upon the Lord and must believe him for the impossible in our lives and the lives of our children. We should at least count the cost of both the advantages and disadvantages of such a practice. We sometimes criticize the schools in the country in which we are working. In fact, the educational system in any country has many subtleties and pitfalls which the devil is constantly using.

5. Bitterness

When we return to an affluent country and see the way people are living, it is easy, almost without knowing it, to become bitter or resentful. We seem to forget that all Christians must learn how to live out their faith in the particular culture in which they find themselves. It is God's will, I am sure, that people throw off certain aspects of their culture and become more Christlike, but this takes time. Our greatest need, when we meet Christians in the midst of their culture, is to be patient and to set an example with our own living.

God leads different people in different ways. We must never forget this when we return to our own countries. When we see the state of some churches and the enormous waste of finance in the home country, it is all too easy to be negative. It is important to try to think positively and to see what the Lord is doing despite some of the problems and difficulties. Our challenging message to God's people should be launched from a positive foundation rather than from a negative or wrong attitude.

6. "The Son of Man Did not Come to Be Served, But. . ."

We make a great mistake when we go home expecting everyone to serve us or treat us as special people. Wherever we are as believers, our burden is not to be served by others, but to serve them. We will be ministered to, but we must get our priorities straight and set proper goals. There are people at home who have suffered more for Jesus Christ and in the work of God than we have out in the field.

We must have real spiritual sensitivity in every situation, realizing that we are in a spiritual warfare, whether at home or overseas. Satan will be constantly attacking. That is why even a so-called vacation or holiday can never be a substitute for true spirituality and the day-by-day walk with Jesus—denying self, taking up the cross and following him. If we are not careful, we find ourselves in a worse condition at the end of our time at home than when we actually arrived. We need to think about serving others; not to constantly expect and desire others to serve us!

7. Feeling Guilty

How easy is it to feel guilty when we enjoy something and when we find life a lot easier than it was in our previous situation. This is an ascetic tendency which can be very dangerous. We need to learn thoroughly how to handle enjoyment and ease; to prayerfully lay it before the Lord. We actually need to learn how to enjoy the good things which the Lord gives. It is a mistake to think that all prosperity is from the devil, because the Lord clearly prospers some people. Imagine what can take place in terms of the work of the kingdom as the Lord takes over the life of a prosperous person.

There is no easy answer to this problem of luxury and ease, and it will be a battle right down to considering what to spend and when to spend it. Once we try to dictate some legalistic rules about this, we are moving into an even greater danger. Part of the challenge of life is to be able to discern, as individuals and as a fellowship, what we should do and how we should react in each situation the Lord positions us. Certainly, without the fruit of the Holy Spirit, whatever we do will have little eternal value.

8. Spending–Spree Materialism

Back home, we can often buy things that are unobtainable or cheaper than they are on the field. People also give us things.

Very soon we find that we are returning with a lot of acquisitions which we don't need, and which can be a stumbling block to those around us. We may expect each of our possessions to be desired by those we are working with and discipling. Once again, it is extremely difficult to find the balance. We need to learn how to resist the urge to buy, while praying about each item with which we return to the field. Here our Christian faith has to become practical. The message that we believe and preach has to be worked into the daily fiber of practical living.

9. Neglecting Prayer and Study

Does a holiday or vacation mean that we neglect prayer and the Word of God? I am amazed that so often when people are on furlough, they do very little to seek out a place where they can attend a prayer meeting with God's people. Although they claim to miss such times of fellowship, they take little initiative to ensure themselves of this privilege.

Our Christian life is truly put to the test when we are more or less on our own, and can, to some degree, do as we please. Of course, it is highly valuable to be totally free for a certain period of time from the field schedule. This does not mean, however, free from the great responsibility to walk faithfully with God. To me, that walk means involvement with God's people in prayer, as well as serious daily worship and study of the Word.

Going Home More Permanently

A friend of mine, who used to be with OM and is now in secular work recently reminded me that most of these principles apply to the person, who returns home for any length of time. It is quite true that after an extensive period in a mission field, or a similar involvement, the readjustment into secular employment and the basic routines of life at home is considerable. It can be even greater than the initial adjustment to field in the first place, since people are more flexible and less set in their ways.

In closing, I am deeply aware that this memo is incomplete. But it is a start. I write as a learner myself, and I'm very much aware of my own needs and failures in many of these areas.

Chapter 19

Whatever Happened to the Prayer Meeting?

Samuel Chadwick, one of God's great men of past years, taught that Satan's greatest aim is to destroy our prayer lives. Satan is not afraid of prayerless study, prayerless work or prayerless religion—but he will tremble when we pray. If Chadwick was correct (and many other great men of God have said similar things), then we have a problem. If there is any part of our church life that seems to be in trouble, it is the prayer meeting. In fact, in an increasing number of churches for all practical purposes, there is no such meeting at all.

There is no lack of books on prayer, and most pastors preach on prayer every now and again. But if there is any doctrine to which we pay only lip service in our churches, it has to be the doctrine of prayer. I have ministered in thousands of churches in Europe, North America and around the world and I have never ceased to be surprised at the neglect of true, heartfelt, corporate prayer. There are some beautiful exceptions of course, but they are few by comparison. I sometimes wonder whether another challenge or message on prayer will do any good. The hour has come for us to pray. Let us put the prayer meeting back into the life of our churches.

Part of my motivation for writing this article came after a weekend of ministry in a church where the mid-week prayer meeting had been dropped, mainly due to lack of interest and attendance. The Holy Spirit worked during that weekend, and in the final meeting on Sunday evening the pastor announced that they would start the prayer meeting again on the following Wednesday evening. Later, I heard that some fifty people had attended and that they had a great time of prayer. The fact that some churches do have good, lively, powerful prayer meetings even in this activistic, leisure-loving, television age is proof that your church can do so as well. But it will take action, discipline and perseverance, combined with large amount of love, patience and spiritual reality.

Some Christians tell me that they have stopped going to dead and badly organized prayer meetings, while others continue only from a sense of duty or guilt. Should we not be drawn into the presence of the living God with higher motivation than this? Why are we attracted only by special speakers and programs, rather than to the Lord himself? What real authority does the Lord Jesus have in our churches today? What authority does he have in your life and mine, if we do not give top priority to meeting regularly with his people to pray?

The Need for Change

To see things change will take both a spiritual and practical revolution. We need a divine combination of practical change and deeper commitment. Pastors spend hours preparing for a sermon, but how much time is put into preparing for the prayer meeting? Linked with this is the great compromise of changing the prayer meeting to a mid-week service or "prayer and Bible study" that involves only ten to twenty minutes of actual intercession after the Bible study and prayer requests. I suppose, some feel this is better than nothing, but many decide that "nothing" is better and so they just don't attend.

Some lively churches with which I have contact, have prayer and Bible study on separate nights in order to give enough time for both. Others have them together, but make the meeting long enough to include at least one hour of prayer. Some hold prayer meetings in various homes, which is good, although often on these occasions there is a tendency for there to be more fellowship than prayer. And when these groups do pray, they often seem to lack reality in the area of intercession.

These functions should not take the place of at least one good church prayer meeting each week at which a large part of the congregation meets. We should follow the example we find in Acts 1:14, *They all joined together constantly in prayer.*

The lack and neglect of such meetings, I believe, are part of the greatest mistakes in our Bible-believing churches, and such deception by Satan represents a far greater enemy than liberal theology or the cults. In fact, a clear study of 2 Corinthians 10:4–7 would show us that prayer is the principal means through which we are going to stand against the enemy whatever way he might attack us. We seem to be blind to the nature of spiritual warfare and feel that as long as we have a full Sunday school and good number on Sunday morning then all is well. Could it be true that if the Holy Spirit left us, very few changes would be made? Would everything go on as usual?

We should be willing to do almost anything to keep from such a deadly state. It seems to be almost too late in some places, where spiritual schizophrenia has set in such a deep level. This will be changed only by radical, deep-rooted repentance. Surely the prayer meeting, and our personal prayer lives, must be of vital importance if anything lasting and real is to take place at the center of church life. Let us put Christ back into his rightful place as Lord of our own lives and of our church programs.

Church Leaders Must Act

The responsibility for action rests with pastors and church leaders, with a need for the cooperation of every church member. It is vital that church leaders meet together for discussion and prayer on specific action, they should take to make the prayer meeting a main event in their churches. Pastors need to realize the importance of firm preaching and teaching on the biblical basis for prayer. They also need to point out some of the things to avoid in prayer meetings: praying too long at one time, preaching at others in our prayers, praying only for the needs of our own church, not changing anything from week to week, judging and looking down on people who pray differently or who lack ability in English or theology, and not really believing or expecting any answers. A lot of good books on prayer are now available and should be widely distributed among the congregation, along with other informative books such as *Operation World*. Church leaders should wait on God and prepare in a serious way so that each prayer meeting is carefully planned and fully used.

Practicality of the Prayer Meeting

As far as the prayer meeting itself is concerned, how can we actively get out of the rut which often makes this the most boring, unpopular meeting of the week? I'd like to pass on a few suggestions used effectively for more than twenty years in our work. We have discovered that to vary the format of the meeting is extremely important, as the more accustomed we become to routines, the less vital it is to us. It can be varied sometimes by beginning with worship, intercession and thanksgiving; other times with a brief challenge to prayer. If ministry from the Word is given, it should be short and yet powerful; individuals could also share specific answers to prayer.

Prayer must involve the mind as well as the heart, as long periods that do not require personal involvement allow the mind to drift. Therefore, it is good to break into groups so that each person is given the opportunity to participate. Each group could, for example, be given information about one area of need and be asked to concentrate their prayers on that.

We use films, videos and DVDs whenever possible and applicable. Many mission groups have produced some very effective ones that are a good stimulus to prayer. When showing a DVD or video, you could stop midway for a time of prayer.

When prayer requests are presented, it is best to keep them short. Long detailed accounts for prayer not only kill the spirit of the meeting, but also often leave very little time for prayer. Items for prayer and praise could be written in advance and given out to people as they arrive, or they could be written on a blackboard. One of the best helps is an overhead projector, especially as outline maps of various countries could also be shown.

Delegate individuals in advance to give a brief update on a particular country. This could include statistics for example, the population of the region, its religion, something of the missionary work being done there, (these and more can easily be obtained from the book, *Operation World*), as well as any current news regarding different situations within that country. If the church has several missionaries, then play short tapes containing up-to-date information about their present circumstances. It may also be a good idea for pastors to encourage people to "adopt" a missionary family; to write to them regularly, and then to present briefly the needs of that family at the prayer meeting from time to time. It would be encouraging for both church members and the missionaries if mission fields could be visited now and again.

Urge different people to pray. Help them to feel relaxed in terms of grammar, theological content or length. Especially encourage those who don't pray very often or not at all, but don't embarrass anyone. There must be a balance between the Holy Spirit's spontaneous work and each person's helping to make the prayer meeting what it should be. Be patient and reject discouragement—people will not learn reality in prayer overnight. In order to encourage people to become more worldwide in their vision, it is good to make use of a world map and other helpful items (like the set of prayer cards available from the address: george@verwer.om.org).

Chapter 20

Conducting Prayer Meetings!

Advanced study, research, and use of computers (as useful as they may be in "missiology") can never be a substitute for fervent prayer on the part of God's people. Hundreds of Scripture verses and dozens of good books attest to the value God attaches to the prayers of his people. His call to us today includes the call to meaningful prayer, both private and corporate. The lack of real, consistent, intelligent group prayer for the unevangelized world—even in many evangelical and Bible-believing churches—should be a great concern to all who love Christ and want his gospel to spread to all nations.

Many Christians really want to be effective in prayer for missions, but are not sure how to begin. Others are finding their own church prayer meetings unattractive, boring, and dead. Even in those groups where there is an exciting, renewed interest in prayer and praise, this does not always include much emphasis on intercession, and especially intercession for world missions. Bible verses such as found in Matthew 9:36–38 are clear in showing the absolutely vital role of prayer in accomplishing the task of world evangelization:

But when he saw the multitudes, he was moved with compassion on them, because they fainted, and were scattered abroad, as sheep having no shepherd. Then he said unto his disciples, The harvest truly is plenteous, but the labourers are few; Pray ye, therefore, the Lord of the harvest, that he will send forth labourers into his harvest.

Laying a Foundation

But what can be done? Stating the facts—even believing in them—is not enough. There must be action! Pastors and church leaders must act, and every church member must cooperate. Here are some basic suggestions which over the years I have observed to be effective:

1. It is vital that church leaders meet together for discussion and prayer on specific action, they should take to make prayer meetings a main event in their churches.
2. There must be loving, firm preaching and teaching on the biblical basis for prayer.
3. There should be wide-scale distribution of good books on prayer to the congregation, along with other informative books such as *Operation World.*
4. Church leaders should wait on God and prepare in a serious way, planning carefully for each prayer meeting.
5. The work of missions can be made more real and personal to individual Christians if church leaders will—
   a. Encourage each one to correspond with missionaries.
   b. Urge families to "adopt" a missionary family and present briefly the needs of that family at the prayer meeting from time to time.
   c. Arrange for visiting missionaries to stay in homes of members of the congregation.
   d. Invite missionaries to share in the prayer meetings as often as possible, arranging for times of fellowship afterwards.

e. Encourage the congregation to visit mission fields and home bases whenever possible.

Specific Suggestions

Now, coming to the prayer meeting itself, how specifically can we get out of the rut which often makes this the most boring, unpopular meeting of the week? I'd like to pass on a few suggestions used effectively for more than thirty years in our work:

1. Vary the format! This is extremely important, as the more accustomed we become to a routine, the less vital it becomes to us. It can be varied by beginning sometimes with worship, prayer, and thanksgiving; other times with a brief challenge to prayer; or with individuals giving specific answers to prayer; or with audio visual materials.

2. Avoid long periods of consistency. Prayer must involve the mind. Long prayers which does not involve personal involvement allows the mind to drift. Therefore, it is good to break the meeting into shorter segments. Here are some ways to do it (these are also given in the previous chapter).

   a. After a time of corporate prayer, break into small groups which will give opportunity for each person to participate. Each group could, for example, be given information about one area of the world and asked to concentrate their prayers on that area.

   b. Make good use of videos and slides/CDs or DVDs. Many mission groups have produced very effective ones which are a good stimulus to prayer.

   c. Present prayer requests, but keep them short. Long, detailed accounts for prayer not only kill the spirit of the meeting, but they also often leave very little time for prayer. Prayer requests could be written in advance and given out as people arrive. Or, they could be written on an overhead projector, or be presented through Powerpoint using maps of various countries, etc.

d. Keep the ministry of the Word short, but powerful.

e. Read quotations from significant missionary biographies or books on prayer.

f. Delegate individuals to give a brief update on a particular field. This could include statistics (population of region, its religion, etc.—all easily obtained from *Operation World*), something of the missionary work being done there, as well as any current news regarding that area.

g. Play short messages from missionaries on the field.

h. When showing audio visuals, why not stop for a time of prayer after a while rather than having a long, non-stop presentation.

i. Do not omit the ministry of music. Good music is an aid in worship and will help set the tone for the entire meeting. During a long prayer meeting, it is important to stop the intercession for a time of "refueling," so to speak, through praise, worship, and thanksgiving.

Frequency and Location

Where and how often should group prayer meetings be held? In addition to the weekly church prayer meeting, I strongly advice that the meeting be periodically held in homes. This opens doors of ministry through the home and avoids the pitfalls of isolating prayer for missions from fellowship and basic spiritual growth.

Around the world, God is working in home meetings. This concept has to be made use of in someway. How sad, on the other hand to see many home groups which have no real interest in prayer for missions.

I believe there should also be spontaneous early morning prayer meetings, lunch time prayer meetings, and days set aside for prayer. Within our work for more than fifty years we have had regular times of extended prayer, often long into the night. I believe this is one of the main factors in the victories we have seen around the world, both with our ships and in our land teams. During these extended time of prayer, people must be made to feel free to leave whenever they wish. They must realize they are not in a spiritual marathon. However, the more information they have about the world's needs, the more responsible they are to pray for those needs to be met.

Remember, we are in a spiritual warfare. Prayer is one of our main weapons and faith is closely linked with it. We must not expect it to be easy. Satan will counter-attack any effort made towards effective prayer. We must avoid any form of discouragement and press on, whatever the cost. Half of the world has still not heard or read the Gospel, and what we do in prayer in God's sovereignty and mercy will be a deciding factor as to whether or not they will. Let us ask God for new ideas and initiatives to be creative in this task that he has given to us. And let us be disciplined in doing our part.

Chapter 21

Denominations or Denominationalism?

As I ministered around the globe over the past 50 years people have repeatedly asked me and written to me about what I am trying to share in this letter. There has been more hurt, disunity and discouragement in connection with this, than we can ever know. Please try and take the time to read what I am sharing, and pass it on to others.

In the ministry of mobilization we are faced with many obstacles and complexities. One of the toughest is the denominationalism which is usually combined with deception and pride.

I am pro–denominations (not all of them), but anti-denominationalism. By that I mean the attitude that makes you believe that yours is the only true church group or at least better than all the others. There is a huge lack of reality and humility among such people, especially now with over 27,000 denominations globally. One group publicly teaches that all others are wrong and the only way is the way they believe and teach. This, of course, becomes cultic and manipulative. There are believers in such groups and we must exercise love and patience, because that is all they know.

It is even more sad that many denominations don't believe that God works much outside their group or local church. By the way, some of the stronger church groups don't want to be called a denomination which is part of their judgmentalism against other denominations. One group recently produced, in their denominational magazine, two articles against what they call para-church agencies making all kinds of false statements. This is especially sad as they have some good churches and lots of wonderful Christians. I find these articles (and they are not new) very divisive and hurtful. It is something that I have noticed around the world for the past 50 years.

Without realizing they write off as second-class, or worse, all:

1. mission agencies
2. most Christian radio and TV programs
3. most Christian camps and youth ministries
4. the Christian film industry and most internet teaching and evangelism
5. most Christian literature and Bible agencies
6. almost all Christian bookshops
7. most Christian conferences/conventions like Keswick
8. most Christian Relief and Development Agencies
9. all international networks like WEA or Lausanne
10. all missionary aviation agencies
11. all ship ministry agencies
12. most evangelistic agencies like Billy Graham and Luis Palau
13. student movements and organizations like UCCF, Campus Crusade, the Navigators
14. Christian Arts and Music ministries
15. most Bible colleges or seminaries and other Christian institutions
16. most drug and alcohol rehabilitation agencies
17. many evangelistic efforts like the Alpha course
    The list can go on. . .

It is almost impossible to honestly maintain such a position, as it denies so much of what God has done over these 2,000 years and what he is doing right now. I know of cases where young people felt the call of God to join a mission event for a summer and were told by their local church leaders that, it could not possibly be of God. Can you imagine the confusion and discouragement that comes from such behavior? As Bible believers we are a minority and are in a narrow way. Why do some get joy of making it more narrow?

The good news is that increasing number of churches and whole denominations believe that most, not all, Christian biblical "so-called" para-church agencies are a vital part of what God, Jesus and the Holy Spirit are doing in the world today. There is only one church and all true believers are part of that church.

Walls have come down when those of us in such groups repent of not more highly esteeming local churches and denominations. I did that publicly once in front of 500 mission and denominational leaders from around the world. One of the most crucial things to remember is that many of the mission agencies are responsible for planting thousands of local churches and even whole denominations, like SIM in Nigeria birthing a whole huge dynamic denomination. We could give many other examples.

I have received beautiful letters from people who have apologized for their attitude toward "para-church" groups and who have changed their viewpoint. As mobilizers, let's get involved in breaking down the barriers and praying for more workers to be released into the harvest. Let all of us who know Jesus and are heaven-bound realize that we need each other.

I submit this hoping that it will increase humility, reality and a great unity of purpose in reaching all peoples with the gospel.

Chapter 22

Facing the Facts

In the task of world evangelization, we are faced everywhere by the need for more workers. The need is never for more open doors. In fact, we are blessed with amazing open doors in so many nations and so many people groups, but nothing is straightforward, and we should never be willing to compromise. Here are a few thoughts from my heart as a result of what I have seen and read over these past 50 years. Luke 14:28 tells us to be realistic and count the cost.

We need to be realistic about the complexities and obstacles that we face. We must resist the temptation to tell wonderful stories and give the wrong impression about the true situation. We need a realistic view of the church. There is a huge variety of local churches with a wide range of opinions and ideas about missions and sending out workers. We should never presume that we are all of one mind.

Churches that were major sending-churches for the last few decades in some cases now cannot keep up with their commitments; in some cases congregations have shrunk or internal problems have consumed time and money. We need to understand that churches are changing.

Some very popular churches have made it known that they don't send out long-term missionaries. They have no money in their budget for missions. They may encourage mission trips in which people pay their own way, or they may pray and give money for projects, or in some cases national workers. Sadly, some even defend their policy by spreading negative stories about the high cost and ineffectiveness of longer term and career missionaries; or they make sure missionary speakers do not get into their pulpits, especially Sunday morning when the people are actually there.

With strong emphasis on the local church, combined with the Western emphasis on paid staff or professionalism, large churches often have large numbers of full time, and paid staff, leaving little money to send out workers.

I am continually stunned by the size of salaries that many pastors receive. This leads to affluent lifestyles and enormous financial demands on the congregation. Though the USA is the heart of this philosophy, it has been for 50 years spreading throughout the world. In my own view this is a great hindrance to world evangelization.

It seems that there is little willingness to sacrifice or forsake anything for the sake of world evangelization. Emphasis on grace and freedom has led to the abuse of grace and a lack of obedience and discipline. We have failed to keep the balance— and I include myself.

I believe that many of our colleges and seminaries have teachers who no longer actually believe that the unreached are actually lost. Various kinds of zeal-killing universalism are on the increase. In fact, in our preaching and teaching today, we seem to hear very little about hell. That is a huge hindrance to mobilizing new missionaries.

Attempts have been made to marry Reconstruction Theology with prosperity teaching to form a new spiritual cocktail, and it is dangerous. Even more balanced holistic messages have led to a de-emphasis of the importance of giving people the salvation message. Many people don't want to give finance, unless it is helping peoples' physical needs. Huge amounts of money go into relief and development (we are speaking of hundreds of millions) while missionaries are held back due to a lack of support. I strongly believe in ministry to whole person, but we need balance.

The truth is that most mission work is carried out where the church already exists. These areas are still crying out for more workers. Only a small percentage of people are working among the unreached or where the church is non-existent. How can this be changed? For 20 years now we have had the great "Unreached Peoples Group Challenge." We thank God for all that has been done, but what about 25 percent of the world's population who have not heard or read the Gospel? We have a long way to go.

Whether it is the "Acts 13 Breakthrough Vision" or something similar or even quite different we long and pray for the church to move into a greater pro-active position in regard to the unreached. We long for trained, anointed and equipped workers to be sent out.

We are in contact with church and mission agencies all over the world and the one thing they all have in common is that they need workers. Most are even praying for those who will come short term and help in the task. The bigger demand is for long-term workers of some level of maturity.

We are in touch with those working in the 10/40 Window and it is clear that thousands of workers are needed there, including those who will go as tentmakers. Most people expected many more to be there by now. I am sometimes asked the question, "Why are there not more workers, especially among the more unreached peoples?"

As we have attempted to work with people around the world, we have discovered many reasons why we are not seeing more workers, especially long-term workers. In my book, *Out of the Comfort Zone,* I speak more extensively on this subject, but I want to briefly list here some of the obstacles. I believe this will help us to better "count the cost" as we are told in Luke 14:25–33 and it will enable us to act and pray more intelligently.

1. Lack of Vision
Only a few seem to actually have the vision in the first place, both of the need as well as the amazing opportunities. Others don't have a vision to send out workers, especially from their own church.

2. Lack of Prayer
Matthew 9:35–38 makes the command about prayer very clear. Despite all the talk and statistics about prayer and some wonderful prayer events and movements, we have to admit that the average church is not a praying church. They may boast of a prayer meeting, but usually only a few people attend and there is often very little prayer for workers and the unreached. It seems that few leaders and believers, and even missionaries, have a disciplined prayer life and ministry. Praise God for every exception and I hope you are one of them, but I am referring to the overall average. Prayer movements have also been invaded by ridiculous and extreme ideas, which have brought division and discouragement to many. Unrealistic expectations created by certain brands of extremism have also left many confused and discouraged. Praise God for his mercy and the way he keeps working in the midst of all the mess.

3. Apathy Among God's People
I think all would agree that this is the overwhelming hindrance to all we want to do for the kingdom. This is one of the reasons, the prayer for revival movements have become such a major emphasis in some places. Occasionally, people have wondered why I sometimes get associated with some people or churches that may seem extreme, and I can only say that I am trying to stay in fellowship with the whole Body of Christ. As someone once said,

(I think it was Brother Andrew) "It's easier to cool down a fanatic than to warm up a corpse!" Someone trying to bring this into balance however said, "Yes, but at least a corpse will not jump up and stab you at the back." I must confess I'm thrilled when I hear of people and churches coming alive and only hope and pray that the people will be disciplined and trained so that they go on as real marathon runners for God! I'm still convinced that a crisis without a process will become an abscess.

4. Lack of Biblical Generosity

Everyone knows that lack of funds is slowing down God's work and certainly hindering the sending of missionaries out for field work. There are powerful exceptions, especially when a localchurch wants to put up a new building. I know that many generous people are reading this and I thank God for you. I know some people are extreme as I was (some would say I still am) as I want to live on the basic essentials and pour everything into world evangelization. By the way, many people believe that without this "extreme" OM might have died in the first couple of years when so little money was coming in. Who knows? All surveys show that only a tiny percentage of money goes outside one's own church and one's own nation. There are powerful exceptions especially for relief and development when there is a huge disaster somewhere. Some even think it is better to send money rather than workers, which again is foolish because it must be both. Let's, in the midst of this, stay grace-awakened and realize that the Lord does lead different people in different ways and let's beware of legalistic judgmentalism.

5. Legalism

God is using his Word and many great books about grace to set people free from this, but it is a long hard road and in many parts of the world, legalism reigns supreme not only in local churches, but in whole denominations. Many feel very threatened by this movement of grace that is taking place. It seems easier to hold God's people together (and we all need loyalty and unity) by the law and all the added "distinctives," which are often just man-made rules and regulations than by grace, love, reality and the freedom of the Holy Spirit. We are also learning the hard way that grace without discipline can often lead to disgrace. Grace does not lay aside basic biblical commandments, but rather brings them into balance and the right priority.

6. Negative Reports

In anything as big as the modern missions movement, there will always be lots of bad news. We know that bad news travels faster than good news and we now have the Web to help. Old-fashioned gossip and misinformation still cause more harm than the Web. I personally have failed in this area and in recent decades have tried to put a greater emphasis on Spirit-controlled speech. Some churches, after sending out one worker, sometimes for only short term, have stopped sending people after their worker came back with a bad report or maybe defeated in his/her own life. It's clear to me that without discernment, grace and forgiveness, there is no way forward.

7. Biblical Compromise

I read a book that showed the drift even on the part of missionaries and leaders away from some of the basics of God's Word. Universalism, used to be considered part of the package of liberal theologians, who did not believe in any case that the Bible was God's Word. But now in various forms, it seems to have invaded our evangelical and biblical communities. Ignorance of the Bible in general seems to be on the increase and that doesn't help. It is not easy as a book lover and publisher to say this, but I must say it. . . some so-called Christian books have done great harm to the work of God and world evangelization. Many seem to be overreacting to extreme brands of fundamentalism and I can sympathize, but we must always be careful of overreacting and acknowledge that because of our own weaknesses and humanness, it is not easy to be totally objective about many of these things. That is one of the reasons we know that real unity in the years to come will be in the midst of great diversity.

I hope these words will drive all of us to our knees. Don't worry about some little thing I have said that you don't like or agree with, but rather be pro-active and ask God what he is trying to say to you personally. We especially pray that people who read this will become more active in reaching the world with the gospel as a goer, a sender, or both. We hope you will link with us in networking with mission mobilizers around the globe.

All of us in this mobilization ministry need a lot of patience. The way ahead will not be easy! We just rejoice over each worker sent forth and each person who comes to Christ. We especially rejoice over each new church planted.

It is harvest time and more churches and people on the field and home are involved in missions than ever before. Of course, Satan is attacking in vicious ways on every level. Let's, more than ever, take the shield of faith and stand against them in the power of the Holy Spirit.

Chapter 23

God's Way to Spiritual Growth
(A message given in the early seventies in India)

I want to begin with two quotations. The first is by C.S.Lewis, from Screwtape Letters:

> We have a tendency to think, but not to act. The more we
> feel without acting, the less we will ever be able to act and in
> the long run the less we will be able to feel.

That is precisely what is happening to the church of Jesus Christ today. For so long, we have not acted on what we have said that now we no longer feel it. That is why the people who really want to do something today are mostly young people. The older generation felt for so long—even to the point of tears without action, without revolution—that now they no longer can act. For 19 years I have preached the Word of God in over 1,500 churches in 30 nations, and I have seen this as the universal disease, exactly what C.S.Lewis describes. It frightens me. It is what I have tried to speak about in my book, *Hunger for Reality*. The double life is something we've got to think about at this convention. If you "get a feeling" for mission;

if you "get a feeling" for Turkey, or Bangladesh or Bombay; if you somehow feel you want to do something, but you don't. Then next year when you come to a missionary conference you'll feel less and some day you'll feel so little you won't even bother to come. That's how the process of degeneration sets in.

The second quote is by J.B.Phillips from *Ring of Truth:*

> Here is the first and most deadly casualty in our modern pattern of thinking. We do not seriously believe God is willing to penetrate the inner springs of human character and begin a solitary revolution there.

This unbelief is our incalculable loss. Two thousand years ago something similar was written by James, in the first chapter of his Epistle: "Be doers of the word, and not hearers only, deceiving yourselves. For if anyone is a hearer of the word and not a doer, he is like a man who observes his natural face in a mirror; for he observes himself and goes away and at once forgets what he was like. But he who looks into the perfect law of liberty, and perseveres, being no hearer that forgets, but doer that acts, he shall be blessed in his doing."

What powerful words! Words that should challenge us to become spiritual revolutionaries for Jesus Christ! That will happen when we allow God's Holy Spirit to begin changing our lives on the inside. As J.B. Phillips said, ". . .allowing God to get right into the inner man."

Now it is very important to understand what I am going to say. We know about the miracle of the new birth, praise God. Have you been born again? Are you sure? Do you know the reality of life-changing, heart-changing faith? It's the only faith the Bible talks about. My Bible tells me nothing about the kind of faith that causes the hearer to raise his hand and say "I believe in Jesus," but doesn't make any change to his life. Do you have a revolutionary faith? I hope so.) But just as the new birth is a miracle, I am convinced that spiritual growth also is a miracle.

We Must Grow!

One of the first countries I worked in was Spain. It is less evangelized than Andhra Pradesh, Assam, Tamil Nadu etc. My first son was born then. When he was small I used to throw him up in the air and catch him. In a few more years he may be taking daddy in his hands! That is the miracle of growth. I believe the need of spiritual growth is often neglected in our thinking. We preach the new birth. We preach various blessings and crisis that can take place after the new birth—and many seem preoccupied with that subject today, but we neglect the doctrine of spiritual growth.

Peter says, "grow in grace and in the knowledge of the Lord Jesus." There is no substitute for spiritual growth. The new birth has to be followed by a process or it will soon become an abscess. Oh, how important it is to understand the need for consistent, continual spiritual growth. And it is because people are not growing that they are not going to the ends of the earth. Before God can thrust you out, he wants to build you up. The great need of today is for intensive spiritual training, whatever way you may get it.

A Training Program

On the ship M.V.Logos we had a training program called the Intensive Training Program. It involved supposedly 14 hours a day of hard work, because each trainee had to read 3,000 pages of Christian literature, listen to so many sermons, 100 tapes, distribute tracts, speak to 100 people about Jesus Christ, spend a quota of hours in the ship's engine room and doing some of the dirtiest jobs on board, and achieve a dozen other goals. Of course, they had five months to do it. We proved that this program works. It is not a guarantee of spiritual life, because only Jesus gives spiritual life; but it can be a tremendous help to people, who for too long have lived undisciplined lives.

e very honest. I learned this from Billy Graham, my
that unless you are ready for a disciplined life then
forget your Christian commitment. You can get blessed in this meeting,
you can be filled with the Spirit, but if you don't learn something of
daily discipline, you'll never amount to anything for Jesus. I have had
young people all over the world tell me, that their problem is that they
do not have disciplined lives. Discipline means doing what you know
you should do rather than what you feel like doing.

Feelings and Faith

I have "Himalayan feelings" that go up and down like a lift! Sometimes
I feel so committed to Jesus Christ. Do you ever feel that way? I love
music—Christian music, powerful words as Larry Norman and others
sing them. I feed on the stuff. When I hear it I feel like shouting,
"The world for Christ! Let's go out on the streets. Let's win souls!" My
feelings soar. Any of you ever had that experience? The next morning,
at 6:00A.M., a brother knocks on my cabin door and I wish I could
choke him! I love sleep. Good old-fashioned sleep! And this fellow
has the nerve to knock on my door at 6:00A.M. and get me out of bed
to run with him one mile. He's mad! I feel totally depressed in the
morning. But I have discovered that God gives victory over feelings.

We need to get up in the morning, and whether you run a mile
or not that's up to you. But get into God's Word, get on your knees
and get with the Lord before you go out and face people, whether you
feel like it or not. I have found that this is a very big thing in my life.

Now, somebody knocking is not enough for me. I have the
arrangement with this brother that when he knocks he stands there
until he sees me. Otherwise, that summon means nothing; I will
just ignore him and go back to bed. But he waits. (The man with
this job is 62 years of age and he's got more energy than most people
on the ship in their twenties and thirties.) I can't leave him standing
there; I have to get up. I open the door, and I want to tell you if you

have to look at me morning after morning, eyeball to eyeball, you'd better get prayer supporters!

Well, I am not depressed every morning of course. I find if I go to bed early it helps. But my feelings are low. I don't want to read the Bible. I don't want to pray. I've been doing it for 19 years and I've read it all. Do I have to read it again? That's why I need a method for breaking my depression. I strenuously exercise my body and run that one mile every morning. (Some mornings I do other exercises; some mornings, to prove I know liberty, I sleep.) I find 90 percent of the time that, when I have finished that mile, my depression has gone.

You can have other methods, but whatever they are you have to learn to overcome living by feelings. There is nothing wrong with feelings. If you feel wonderful, fine. I often do. But you can't trust feelings. You can't put confidence in feelings. It must be in God's Word. The Lord himself said, "If any man would come after me, let him deny himself and take up his cross daily and follow me." He doesn't say, "If any man comes after me and feels like taking up his cross. . . ." The vast majority of Christians I believe, are having a great problem because they have never learned how to deal with their feelings.

Guilt and Grace

There are many feelings that hinder us in spiritual growth and none more than the guilt feeling. It is my belief that many of our churches today are legalistic. We have a Christianity too often of rules and regulations. Do this; don't do that. I'm not saying there are no rules in the Christian life. There are rules. But you don't grow in your spiritual life by keeping the rules. You don't grow by determining that you are never going inside a cinema, or you are not going to do this thing or that thing. You grow through communion with God and feeding on his Word. You grow as you draw upon the promises of God.

As you grow there will be failures. Sometimes sin will catch you, and of course this will be your own fault. But I John 1:9 says, *If we confess our sins, he is faithful and just to forgive us our sins and to cleanse us from all unrighteousness.* Praise be to God! That's the only reason I'm here. In my process of growing these 19 years, especially in the early years, I have failed so often. Not with sins that bring about scandal, but the "little sins" that are big in God's sight and bring discredit in heaven. And that is my concern for you. You will never grow, you will never be mature, if you do not learn to deal with guilt.

But praise God for guilt! Guilt is necessary, but it should lead immediately to repentance, to the cross, to the forgiving grace of an all-loving God. And then the guilt is washed away. Sometimes, especially for Christian leaders, there must be a confession of sin to others so that our relationship may be put right and our service be effective. But basically when we come alone to God with repentance and confession, he cleanses us. Are you clean today? I can't talk to you about missions if you are not right with God. I can't talk to you about world missions if there is guilt in your heart because of unconfessed sin, or because you doubt God's grace. You may have repented; you may even have confessed your sin and put it right with your neighbor, but if you doubt God's promises of forgiveness then you are allowing Satan to grip you in a guilt complex.

For Example, Sex

If there is any area in life where we are phony it can be in the area of sex. I have had people tell me, "Now brother George, this is India and not New York. We don't talk about sex in the church." But the Bible was not written by a Texan or a Londoner; it is an Eastern book. This book speaks about sex over 100 times and shows God's answer for sex problems—what we can and cannot do. And it speaks about the beauty of sex within marriage, and its ugliness and defiling power outside marriage. I have got more feedback on this subject than any other I have preached on. I am convinced that often the worst effect of sin in this area is the deep guilt-scar it leaves. Somehow we do not allow God to heal us here.

Until you get your sex life disciplined, even just within the mind, and until you get your sex life under the control of the Spirit of God, he will not be able to use you the way he wants to. That means discipline, growth, and realizing what to do if you do sin. It means reality and revolution.

I'll never forget listening to Billy Graham preach at the Urbana Missionary Conference in 1957. It shook me. I was a young Christian and I had many struggles. He said, "Young person" (he was addressing 6,000 young people), "if you lose the sex battle, you have lost all." And I would beg of you teenagers and young people to discipline your life, to determine to stand against the wiles of the devil, to flee youthful lusts in whatever form they come to you. That means the books you read, the pictures you look at. I want to keep my eyes off from anything that is going to create the wrong subconscious drives in my life, because the big attack of Satan is on the subconscious mind. Everything you have ever seen or read is recorded in your subconscious mind.

All over India in the visits of the Logos we have seen young people coming into victory, not through some little short cut, but through God's program of training and discipline. In Kerala, a young man came to me. He had been involved in Christian work in his college and now came to me for counseling. He began, "Mr. Verwer, I have a problem—dancing."

"Dancing!" I said. "Well, I would not consider that a major problem. It isn't the best thing for Christians to do and I am sure you can overcome it." So, we talked and talked, and finally he broke down and said, "I am a practicing homosexual." (The Bible speaks quite a bit about that problem.) And he just shook.

Apparently a university professor had seduced this young man into homosexual practices (which are going on more than any of us will ever know). He had been converted only some months before. Now he shared his failure with me, confessed it and repented. I had the privilege of corresponding with that man and see him go on in victory. There is victory even for problems as serious as this one, because God is love, God is merciful, God forgives.

I am praying that you will determine with all your heart to let the miracle of spiritual growth take place in your life. God will work if you want him to. You can grow. You can live the disciplined life. You can be an effective soul winner. You can be a missionary in Turkey, in India, in Bombay etc. God can use you. But you've got to determine daily to deny self, take up the cross and follow him. That is God's way. It isn't easy, but it is his way.

Chapter 24

Reasons Why Workers Leave the Field

1. The most important is that God has led them to go for mission work. God often changes our direction and incorporates all of our humanness in it. I urge you to read Viv Thomas' book, *Second Choice*. Even if someone returns because of sin, failure or some other negative factor, God can still overrule especially if there is reality, brokenness and repentance.

2. Poor leadership on the field is another reason people "don't make it" and it is why one of our main ministries must be training and formation of godly, gifted leadership which must be combined with helping new believers understand the biblical basis of leadership. There is much abuse and confusion on this subject and so many believers are confused.

3. Equally important is unrealistic expectations. As a book publisher I must confess that often it is books that create this unrealistic expectation. We have too many books with nice formulae and not connected with some of the things we hear or read about. Godly, gifted leaders are still sinners, saved by grace and will continue

to sin and fail. We must be ready to forgive and grow together in repentance and brokenness. Leaders have to make hard decisions and with the range of people in most teams, there is always someone who is not happy. This sometimes leads to gossip and soon you will have a mess. If I did not believe that God could work even in the midst of our people-made messes, I think I would become permanently discouraged (I would love to send you my message on discouragement).

4. Failure in the sexual area is another reason why people return from the field. I could tell some "horror" stories. Pornography, especially on the Worldwide Web, is causing major damage in frontline mission work. Not many are willing to openly talk about it, much less really do something about it. People sometimes face loneliness on the field and this can set them up for a quick romance (not from God) that ends in disaster. I urge people to read books on this subject like *The Snare* by Lois Mowday and *When Good Men Are Tempted* by Bill Perkins. Unfortunately, leaders are often the enemy's targets in this aspect of the spiritual warfare. That is why marital problems often cause people to return home.

5. Personality, strategy and doctrinal conflict are also near the top of the list that send people running home for cover. On the practical level, there never seems to be enough time to sort everything out and often leaders are on overload and on the way to "burnout." How did so many "grace killers" get on the mission field? Everyone should read Charles Swindoll's, *The Grace Awakening*.

6. Failure in the areas of language and cultural learning and adaptation are part of important factors. Again, I want to affirm that for 46 years I have seen all kinds of people used on the mission field; so let us be slow to judge, especially in regard to what God is doing or not doing. If people are learners and are willing to receive correction and keep growing, then there is always hope. Humility and true servanthood can often make up for shortfall in language

and other areas. The abuse of grace can also come in and I think we all know that "grace without discipline can lead to disgrace" and that in turn can hamper the work in very real ways.

7. The lack of teamwork and pastoral care are another major factors. Many agencies have improved in this in the past years, but my conviction is that without 1 Corinthians 13 reality, nothing will really work. We need people who have proved the reality of God's grace in their lives especially, before they get into long-term missions. Short-term missions done in the right way can often be a great step in that direction. Some short-term work just helps people put their sins and difficult ways cemented. That is why it is so good when the discipleship process begins at a very young age. I believe that Teen Street camps are helping with this as well as other similar events (www.teenstreet.org).

8. Problems and complexities at home. In the days of email, etc. people on the field are still involved at home. Splits and other problems in their home churches affect them and often leads to drop in their support or they are asked to return.

9. Shortage of support or difficult financial pressure. Many never go in the first place, because they hate raising support or are unable to raise it. This is a major factor that again we don't like to honestly talk about. The problems and complexities are endless and it's where I need a fresh baptism of godly optimism. Please listen to my message, "Does the Lack of Funds Hinder God's Work?"

10. Satan and his forces are another reason. We don't want to over-emphasize the devil, but there are many strong verses about him and we know he militantly opposes world evangelization. He especially loves to sow legalistic and wrong views of God himself. We are told that he sometimes comes as an "angel of light" and a roaring lion seeking whom he can devour. This is why a basic Spirit-filled walk with God, or whatever term you want to call it, is the most important way to stay in the center of God's will.

Chapter 25

Recruiting
the Right Way and the Wrong Way
(An Interview in 1982 with Evangelical Missions Quarterly)

The interview was conducted at Keswick, N.J., after the IFMA meeting. What follows is an edited version of the transcript. My replies, cover a lot of territory and include some provocative thoughts. After discussing OM's methods, I went on to share insights about youth today, American culture, and what churches, families, and mission agencies can do to recruit and train more young people for overseas ministries.

What is your basic recruiting pitch?
Verwer: "A very strong message from the New Testament. Jesus said, 'Go.' Therefore, all should search their hearts about where they should go as witnesses. For some, it may be locally, but everybody should be going; everybody should be a witness. Acts 1:8 is very important in our thinking. We bring out the challenge of training, whether or not you are planning to be a missionary. Maybe you are thinking about being a pastor, or about working for IBM. That doesn't matter. What is important for young people is to get some

training overseas. They should get to know people of other culture, and gain an understanding of the world of people in a biblical context. They should serve the Lord and help the church.

We try to show young people, there's a job they can do. Young people aren't just to sit for another five years and somehow arrive where we are. Many young people do not feel that their faith is real. It's just in their head. But if the right challenge is given to them, the right opportunity, they respond to trust God for something. We teach them about seeing definite answers to prayer. Many young Christians have never seen specific answers to prayer. When they start seeing this, you get more response and more growth."

Why have you been so successful in recruiting?
Verwer: "We don't think of ourselves as being so successful. We feel that we should have had a lot more people. It's been a lot harder than we thought, in the sense of trying to train people for some countries, that are especially on our hearts, like the Muslim world. We have had some success. We have 700 people now committed to working in the Muslim countries and among Muslims. That, to us, is a great answer to prayer. That is where the secret lies—prayer. The Word clearly says that if we pray to the Lord of the harvest, he will send forth laborers. Our success is usually not because of any one thing. Together, it is the mercy of God, prayer, the individual's response, and spending time with young people. This is very important in our fellowship. We place very high emphasis on relationships. If we do not get our relationships sorted out—learning how to live together and understand one another, being loyal to the leader, and the leader learning how to relate and love and minister to people—when we get out to these countries we will come apart. There will be disunity and confusion. Spiritual revolution and world evangelism will grow out of right relationships, first with God and then with our coworkers."

Are you saying that you do not have a specific recruiting method?
Verwer: "I don't think we do. We have structure, of course. People come with us for a summer and if they are happy and we are happy, they move on with us for a year. If they seem to be growing and they want to stay another year, they can. Others, however, come in through the back door. They may go right to the ship. They may be recruited in some port, though they have to get their church background. They have to get references. They have to go through our books and tapes. Some of these back door recruits go to the ship rather quickly, to be an engineer or a captain. This has revolutionized their lives. I think of a missionary with Overseas Missionary Fellowship. He started as a second officer on our ship. He met his wife on our ship and now they are out as missionaries with OMF. The man who used to be our plumber is now a missionary in Nepal. Working-class people have been neglected by missions. We have tended to recruit from the intelligentsia and from the universities. We have neglected a great mass of practical people, yet they are needed in mission work. Often, after they have used their practical skills, they develop other ministries.

We found that if you give people step one, steps two, three, and four will follow. So many young people and even older people are not getting step one. The obstacles are too big. We put up all the scholastic and other requirements before they can take step one, so they do not get to step two and step three. Then we sit back and wonder what is happening."

Speaking of requirements, what minimal requirements do you have?

Verwer: "You have to know Jesus Christ. You need to be born again and really know it. You have to have a reference from your church, that you are a person who is growing and who is willing to learn. Once you are in, that doesn't mean that you will go where you think you want to go. If you are only a year old in Christ, and you're just beginning to learn, you are probably not going to go to India, or Sudan. If you are interested in Turkey, you may go to Berlin and work among Turks. Most likely, you may end up in the packing department at the literature base in London. There, the job you are doing with your hands isn't the main thing, though that is important. The main things are the nights of prayer, the Bible study program, building relationships, learning, reading books, seeing films, the total exposure to a committed community. Next year, if you are ready, you may go to India."

Have you modified your recruiting methods in any significant way over the last 25 years?

Verwer: "In the first years in Europe we recruited too many. We try to be more careful now. We do a lot of interviewing right along the line, two or three or four interviews, before people go to the country that they sense they should be going to. Also, our ship is now a training base for people praying about some of these other countries and about other mission societies. We felt from the very beginning that we must be totally international. We must live on an equal level with the people in any country where we are working. The Mexicans, the Spaniards, and now Malaysians and Indians they can come into the work, they can go to other countries, they can be involved in decision-making processes of the fellowship.

This is one of the reasons why we are having an enormous response. Full-time workers backed by their churches, trusting God for finances, from Argentina, Mexico, Korea, Singapore and Malaysia. We are not talking about a few dozen, we are talking about a couple of hundred people, who make up a major force within OM. This is providing new life to the whole body.

Another significant change is our very large force from continental Europe, which in the 1950's was not a major sending area. Today Germany is our largest growing sending field. Amazing things are happening also in Sweden and Finland. Norway is growing. Now Australia is getting involved. There is tremendous potential in Australia for India and that part of the world."

To get more specific: How and where do you find these people? Through radio, television spots, literature? Do you have a couple of hundred recruiters living out of suitcases? Do you send musical groups?

Verwer: "The greatest publicity, we believe, is a holy life. When a young person has this training, and has come into an understanding of the lordship of Christ and a walk with Christ—we hope in a very down-to-earth way, not in a super-spiritual way—he is our best recruiter. We have very, very few men in full-time recruiting anywhere in the world. Most people have a number of ministries. I have been recruiting, but it's not really my first ministry. My first ministry is the oversight of the whole work, worldwide, which mainly means relationships with all the leaders, who are really doing the work. But all of us are available part time for people whom the Lord is touching about joining and getting involved in missions, whether it is with OM or not.

Another major thing: we do use literature, filmstrips, and public meetings. Throughout the world we have thousands and thousands of meetings every couple of months. I myself take 500 meetings a year. That includes teaching–meetings among our own people. We try very much to work as a team and not emphasize personalities."

I am just projecting here, but I think one possible factor in your success in recruiting is what OM itself has to offer. Do you agree?

Verwer: "That is probably true. In fact, now that I think of it, a lot of young people have told me, that is why they came. They heard that it was a bit tough—the discipline, prayer, and doing evangelism.

We have scared some away, I can assure you, but the ones who come generally mean business. They're challenged by the toughness of the task, the size of the obstacles. The key word in OM is the title of my book, *Hunger for Reality*. Most of them have come because they've seen this reality in people's lives, and it's attractive to them and they stay on."

What do you look for in your screening process that would disqualify a person?

Verwer: "There are not many people who are disqualified. As long as they know that they are coming for basic training and they are willing to learn, not many are disqualified. But we watch out for religious extremists, people who are very extreme in their doctrinal positions. We don't feel they are able to relate to young people, even in the training period, so they have to read a book called, *Revolution of Love and Balance*. One of the chapters is called, "Extremism." After they go through our tapes and books, a lot of people just don't come. If they've got a reasonable amount of emotional stability, if they are ready to be learners, if they know Christ personally, and if their church or some group of Christians is standing with them, usually they get a green signal. On top of that, they all have to see the Lord provide some finance, and that is a big obstacle, even though our figure for the summer is quite low."

Every mission has so many jobs that they are looking for people to fill. Does OM say we need so many engineers, so many book packers, so many street evangelists, for example, and then go out to find people to fill those slots, or do you just assign people after you recruit them?

Verwer: "We have certain jobs open right now. I need an accountant for the literature operation in London. We might bring him in through the back door in a crash course to get him there, but that's the exception. That would represent maybe 10 percent of the people who come on. Most people have to begin with the basics. Of course, we like to find out what their qualifications are. We are very people-oriented, but first we want to see them growing, to become Christlike individuals. That is our priority. If we are going to reach the world for Christ, people need to be trained in evangelism. They're going to go out into the streets; they are going to sell Christian books; they are going to do personal work; they're going to learn how to deal with people. Everything must be secondary to the basic spiritual training in prayer and evangelism."

You seem to be very much in touch with the youth culture and the way kids feel today. They want to find a mission that will take them with their talent, their training, their skill. You seem to be saying that OM encourages the youth tide at this point.

Verwer: "You've touched on one of the greatest problems in missions. Young people are under this pressure, often by parents, by our whole system, by the fear of never having a job and all other kinds of things. Most of the young people from the United States settle back in their own country. In the United States, the religious situation is so huge, there is so much money, that almost anybody can get a job and still be serving the Lord. That is not true overseas. Overseas, many things that are done by professional Christian workers have to be done by a layman who holds down a job.

It's a different world from what they're used to in the USA That's why we want people, who can develop adaptability and flexibility. We're making a serious mistake, giving these young people all these trainings. Then, they get a wife and several children before they ever get to the field. They cannot adjust. Because the missionaries have all these knowledge, the nationals feel very inferior. Often, we send people to India who are not that superior, intellectually. They get on very well with the Indians and the Indians are asking us for more people like that. We have never met a "go home" spirit in the history of our work. We're making a mistake by overeducating the people, who go to the field. We need to get them to the field sooner, so they can develop flexibility, adaptability, and of course, spiritual life. Some of them may need more education later on, to fit special situations, but by then they should have a little humility."

You said that mission recruiters turn off more young people than they recruit. What are they doing wrong?

Verwer: "The best Christian in the world is going to turn off some people; I've turned off people. When we turn off young people it's because we lack enthusiasm. How can a person talk about the greatest thing Christ has ever given us to do without a little enthusiasm? Maybe I'm extreme, because I am too excited. In England, I try to keep a low profile, but even the British respond to somebody who has an enthusiastic and exciting approach about mission work. It's one of the most exciting things a young person can ever do.

Another reason is that we overemphasize qualifications: How dedicated you have to be! you've got to have your prayer life together; you've got to have this and you've got to have that. We fail to communicate that these are our goals, and that as we start growing we take steps of faith, we launch out into the deep. We seem to give the idea that the missionary is somebody special with something extra. It's a mistake to give the idea that the missionary is somebody extra-disciplined, extra-spiritual. The average person can't relate to that. In general, young people are turned off to missions."

Do you see any trend in culture that makes it hard to recruit people for missions?

Verwer: "I see tremendous materialism. People are used to living an easy life. Young people have everything they want, except of course, the things they can't buy: emotional peace and joy. But look at the soft life of materialism. Bible schools are giving better food; they have less rules; they have better accommodations: telephones in the rooms, television sets down the hall. It's tough to go and recruit people out of this and convert them into a spiritual guerilla force, ready to live on the barest essentials, ready to suffer for Christ, ready to spend hours in the street in hard evangelism in tropical countries, willing to live with people of different nationalities, eating foods they don't like. I mean, you're talking about a whole new world. That's why it takes years to wean people off this culture."

Looking back over 25 years, do you see anything that if you had it to do over again, you would do differently?

Verwer: "Yes, I would have listened to people more and tried to find out more where they were coming from. I would have developed a broader lifestyle. I maintain my convictions with love and patience, but I can't push them on other people. Spiritual balance has enabled OM to move into places and win people. God doesn't lead the French Church the same way he leads the American Church. God works within the context of a person's culture. The Christian life is so big that no one person, and certainly no one group, has all of it. We are all learning. We are all growing."

What contribution has OM made to the established, traditional mission agencies?

Verwer: "Believe me, from my earliest days, I've always had a great respect and appreciation for other missions. I've always felt it was a miscommunication, part of my own fault, that certain missions felt threatened by OM. Whenever people got to know us, and realized our attitudes and our convictions, there was an immediate link up. We've been linked with many other missions on the field for 20 years. Sometimes people back home don't even know what is going on between the people who are on the front lines together. We cannot afford separations between missions. We should not tolerate disunity.

I'm not sure what our contribution to other missions should be. We've got a lot of weaknesses in our own movement. We are still a fellowship of learners. There is so much unreached ground, that we're not sure what our ministry to other fellowships should be. One thing, we do have a lot of contacts, a lot of literature, and a lot of films available in many languages. We're in 500 literature projects right now. We want to plug in to any society that can be involved. We also want to be involved in revival of prayer. Perhaps we can help others by setting the pace in prayer—nights of prayer, prayer emphasis days, prayer for world missions, prayer for workers to go out to the new frontiers, prayer for older workers to be encouraged. Maybe the Lord wants to use us a little bit to call the whole church back to the basics: the lordship of Christ, the cross, love for one another, prayer, evangelism."

I'm sure you're doing a lot of thinking about the future. Are you satisfied with the number of recruits you are getting? Would you like to increase the number?
Verwer: "Our leaders do not have total unity about this. Some feel that our numbers should go way up. We have tried to keep our growth at a slow steady pace, because we feel that our pastoral care is very important. If we get too many at one time, we're going to fail. We've had some serious failures, so we seem to be adding 50 or 100 more a year for the longer term, on the year program. We could absorb more in the summer."

One of the hot debates in missions is the question of short term vs career service. Is short-term service really a cop out for a life-time career commitment?
Verwer: "A lot of the people who went out in the past for a life-time

career never went back for their second term, so in effect they were short term. Because of our overemphasis on life-time commitment, those people suffered for years from incredible guilt and other difficulties. When we talk about career, we like to talk about the successful ones, those great missionaries who stayed for 30 and 40 years. I feel inferior to such people and I'm ready to tie their shoelaces, but they do not represent the whole picture.

There are strengths and weaknesses in both approaches. We need both. Our ultimate goal is to see long-term career missionaries. There are several thousands who are on long-term Christian service, as a result of getting involved in OM's short-term training program. That's proof that two things can fit together. However, it is important that the short-term work be a priority. It can't be a little second thought, just because everybody else is starting. Armies fight with a large percentage of short-term soldiers and a small percentage of career officers. In world missions we need a greater balance, so that we get an army of men and women, especially single men and women, giving two, three, or four years. Many of our people stay four years. Many postpone marriage in order to do it."

One of your requirements is that a recruit has to bring support. How does this affect your recruiting?
Verwer: "Missions are not realistic enough. Many young people want to go, but their churches are not going to support them. Also, a lot of young people don't have what it takes to go around to 20 different churches, especially Europeans. There've got to be different alternatives. We have chosen one road, but we don't feel that's the only road. We can learn from each other. Our short-term army of single men and women live on relatively little. They live in teams. There are all kinds of places to live if you're flexible. Families, of course, demand a lot more. So once a person in OM has a family, he's

got to see some breakthroughs in answer to prayer. He may have to spend some time with his home church. We emphasize building an in-depth relationship with a few churches, so they will feel a vital part of the ongoing thrust. We also have tentmakers, who support themselves by their own income. We've got to be very flexible in raising support. At the same time, we've got to teach young people how to pray. If God isn't God, then everything we're doing is ridiculous. But if God is God, he will supply finance."

As you talk to hundreds of young people, what are their chief problems?

Verwer: "One of the biggest is low self-image. Their parents often have been very effective in reminding them of their failures, which isn't the greatest way to encourage people. A large segment of youth are perfectionists and idealistic. Strong Bible pulpits have painted an image of a Christian that's near perfect.

An increasing number is mixed up sexually. They've been in perversion. Every youth audience has some people who have been in perversion and who may still be in it. There are many, even in seminary and Bible college, living a double life—prostitutes, homosexuals, etc. We must deal with the problems of sex. Can you be a missionary if you lust and haven't got 100 percent victory? Do missionaries ever have these problems? Why is it not talked about more? As we deal with the issue biblically, a lot of people are going to be set free. Some of our greatest workers are people who would not be in missions if someone had not helped them with the real issues in their lives. We missionaries are sinners; we've got our problems, and even on the mission field we sometimes fail."

What is the role of the family and the church in recruiting? You have said that sometimes parents get in the way. How can

the family and the church help to get more young people out to the field?

Verwer: "When it comes to the family and the church, there's a lot of ignorance about missions, the importance of missions, and a failure to see missions as part of the total counsel of God. This very important aspect of biblical truth, which must not be separated from other truths, is being left out. This is one of the greatest problems in America: Missions is considered an optional extra. It is considered important by a lot of Christians, but it's separate. Rather than incorporate a strong missionary thrust into the basic weekly teaching of the church, we have a missions conference. We should have both.

Every believer should be interested in missions. Missions needs to be brought into the mainstream of teaching and church life and right into our homes.

We can bring missions into our family devotions by using missionary prayer letters and pictures of missionaries. We should entertain missionaries passing through. They have an enormous influence on our children. The devil has almost blinded us. There is a lack of sanctified imagination about how we can motivate our young people. Get them involved. You would think that parents would want to have their young people get involved in something like OM in Europe. Often, that is not the case. They are threatened by it. What if little Johnny doesn't get his engineering degree? Parents are laying on this pressure to be somebody in our society. The thing really gets out of control."

What about a missionary call?

Verwer: "There has been an overemphasis on the emotional type of call. There has been a lack of clarity about what a call really is. A lot of teaching about the will of God is extreme. I don't think the will of God is easy to find. There is an element of risk in life.

Young people have to be taught to step out by faith. I've always had a nagging doubt about a lot of things I've done. We overemphasize the missionary call: 'Make sure you have a call. If you go out there on your own steam, you're going to end up in a mess. If you sit back here and miss God's plan for lack of initiative and vision and faith, you may get into a mess.'

Guidance is a better word than call. Young people need guidance. They need teaching about guidance. God leads different people in different ways. Some are less emotional than others. The church should play a more vital role in this."

What should mission agencies be doing to get more recruits?

Verwer: "We need to get more people involved in recruiting. All of us who are in recruiting, who are middle-aged or older, need to get a number of Timothys and train them. We must train them how to multiply their faith, which is a term I prefer to recruiting. When I was only 17, I was taking youth meetings. I don't get asked to take those meetings today. Probably, they don't think I would be free. I take some, but OM has a second level of people in their twenties and even younger, spreading the vision: Telling people what it's like and directly challenging them to get involved in something within the next 12 months.

Linked with this, we've got to release finance, so that some of these young people don't have to work in the summer to get back into our expensive schools, but instead can get into on-the-field training overseas, or in some cases cross-culturally within our own country. We should use literature more. We need a great wave of distribution of powerful missionary books and cassettes.

To get more recruits will mean getting rid of some excess baggage. It will mean a lot more prayer. As God does a deeper work in us, it makes us more attractive for Christ. As we meet with young people, we're going to be able to relate to them, and the Holy Spirit is going to touch their lives. We don't have to worry about how old we are. We can touch people, who are much younger than we are, if we're young at heart."

NB–Please check OM websites in your country to see how to join in your country. www.om.org

Chapter 26

Revolution of Balance

Have you ever wondered what the real burden of OM leaders is for those who are only in OM for a year or two? There are moments when it is thought that all we want is sweat, tears, a pile of tracts distributed, and many sermons preached. A brief eavesdropping on a 3 Day Coordinators' Conference would enlighten you; for every year the Lord has broken us as leaders of the Movement and shown us our many failures. Actually, our main desire for each one of your lives is spiritual balance.

Often we hear people in OM refer to certain matters as "this is the way it is done in OM." Certain people are described as being "typically OM." Yet what is typically OM? I want us to look together at some truths that are often neglected. In this way I hope we will see what OM really believes and what OM really wants, that we may begin to work at putting some of these areas straight in our own lives.

Discipleship in a Secular World

Spiritual balance is something that must be real for each of us.

If one only understands the principles superficially, then one will quickly find that the principles will not stand the test of the secular world. It is my deep conviction that discipleship is not just for full-time workers. Discipleship is for every believer. Discipleship is not just for people who are living in a community like we do on an OM team, or even on the Logos. It is for people everywhere. Discipleship is not a set of rigid rules. The principles of discipleship are more flexible and adaptable than many of us would dare to admit. One set of Bible truths taken to extreme without the balancing truths of another set can lead people into frustration. Frustration will never lead to spiritual reality. I really want us to have a balance in our spiritual truth.

Groups Outside OM

Have strong convictions, but be flexible and adaptable as a person. These truths are for all balanced Christians, not just for OMers. There are many people outside the OM fellowship, who know more about these principles than many of us inside! There is a great danger that being in OM makes a person believe he's got these things when he doesn't. Sometimes people who have never heard the teaching of OM are living it, and respond enthusiastically when they do hear some of it.

The disciple, though he has strong convictions, is flexible and adaptable. His cardinal rule is LOVE. When he goes into a situation with which he disagrees violently and wants to war and stamp his feet and cry out and preach, love restrains him. Love should cause him to think before he speaks. Most of us realize our tongues run faster than our brains, and this gets us into much difficulty. The true disciple, though he has strong convictions, is adaptable and flexible.

Sometimes messages you hear build up strong convictions on minor issues as well. If you join another group, you may find they have different convictions. Unless you are flexible, adaptable and loving, you will not be able to fit into another fellowship easily. When a person feels he can only stay in one group, he is shown to be unbalanced.

Several times I thought, I would like to join the Salvation Army. They are about as different in certain areas, as any group can be from basic OM beliefs. Yet, reading about them gave me a great desire to work with them, in spite of the areas in which we would not agree.

There is nothing wrong with a strong conviction if you realize you are a learner. Without that flexibility and adaptability, your convictions will dig your own grave. This is particularly true in the tough secular world.

High Aims

Have high goals, yet accept yourself completely. Many messages have been given on the subject of self-acceptance, although they may have been called different things. Yet it is very easy for us not to remember or even to grasp the message, though we have heard it a number of times. The devil is a specialist in deceitfulness. The tendency is for us to judge others, to see the faults in others rather than in ourselves. When we hear powerful messages, we tend to see the weaknesses in other people and to think we ourselves are doing fairly well, when this is not so.

OM has higher goals in some respects than some other Christian groups. These goals can make us into neurotics. Some Christians become neurotics because they aim at impossible standards. Christians tend to aim and accept fantastic goals that either kill them or so distress and discourage them that they backslide.

With our high goals and high aims we must have complete self-acceptance. We must have that deep inner peace, because we are accepted in the beloved even when we are groveling in the mud because of our own mistakes. It is a difficult balance to find and there is a great danger of neurosis.

We must have high goals. Let us aim high. Mr. Fred Jarvis says, "The great sin of Christians is not failure, but aiming too low." We should aim as high as we can. Even on the ship, one of the problems is that we aim too low. We must aim high with complete self-acceptance; then, when a mistake is made we do not heap self-pity on ourselves and drown in the mire of discouragement and despair, but rather maintain a true spiritual balance.

The Discipline of Rest

The third spiritual balance is to have strong discipline while being relaxed and rested. It is important to be strong in both areas. There must be times when you throw yourself into difficult situations, releasing the greatest amount of energy and discipline, and there must be times when you throw yourself into being carefree and relaxed, floating on top of the world. Without both of these seeming extremes, you are not going to make it.

Some will ask, "Are we not supposed to be soldiers all the time?" Yes, but even a soldier does not keep his finger on the trigger all the time. A real soldier is a person who knows how to relax. When he relaxes, he builds up his physical strength and power, so he can go on to battle and accomplish more in a week than he would have done in a month. Billy Graham recently stated that if he could live the last 10 years of his life over again, he thinks he would give himself completely to the battle and then retreat—giving himself to the Word, prayer and rest. Some think OM teaches we should never take a holiday, we should never relax for a moment, but this is not true. We must take it easy at times. A violinist tightens up his strings before playing a concerto, but when it is over, he releases them or they would snap. In other words, we should learn to come apart or we will literally COME APART.

For our health, as well as our spiritual life, it is important to learn to relax. Different people do this in different ways. Some people need complete separation from work to relax. Some need a week's holiday, and others can just take off a few hours, or even change their job and be relaxed. Other people's attitude towards their work enables them to work in a relaxed way and never become as up tight as some others. Because we know so little of relaxation you will hear me preach more on the rest of faith than on discipline, though I believe in both equally.

Concentration without Frustration

Fourth, we need concern without neurosis. Recent studies suggest that evangelical Christians with a strong Protestant outlook tend towards neurosis. It is healthy to have a concern that things are done right and people are living right without becoming neurotic. Let us have peace within ourselves when things are going wrong. Having a sort of itch, a psychological compulsion which does not come from above, but from one's ego, is neurosis. Actually we should not be afraid of a little bit of neurosis, and in fact most of us have some. The modern psychologists suggest we throw away our Protestant ethic with ideas such as, "You can't have sex before marriage" because this makes us neurotics. But, as another psychiatrist recently stated, "The Victorian Ethic has produced a generation of neurotics and the Twentieth Century Liberty Ethic is producing a generation of psychotics." A psychotic is ten times worse than a neurotic. We should be neither.

It is important to keep our rooms clean and tidy. If someone sees rubbish lying around, it is good to get rid of it. However, the neurotic is bothered if there is one speck of dust. He will not be able to live very easily anywhere because he is so bothered about getting rid of all the tiny specks of dust. Eventually he will burn up inside and continually move around, unable to settle at anything because of his neurosis. (This is often true in marriage also.)

Many perfectionists have neurosis. In the book, *None of These Diseases,* we see this brought out clearly. Perfectionists crack, or else, cause a lot of other people to crack.

Perfection through Failures

Fifth, our goal is perfection while learning to handle shortcomings and failures. To be perfect, should be the goal of every true Christian: to live a life in the Spirit, to not offend anyone, to have maximum love, to do all things right and to glorify God in every action. This is spiritual perfection and this should be our goal.

Each of us must come to a place where we are able to accept failure, especially our own failures, mistakes and shortcomings. Often the Christians have such high standards for themselves that when they miss the mark, they don't know what to do. They become so totally frustrated that they wallow in self-pity and take a long time to get back to the beginning again. They will repent, believe that God has forgiven them, but actually live in a form of purgatory as they believe that, if they chasten themselves emotionally and mentally for a certain number of days, they will be able to get back onto the same spiritual plain.

Other Christians live a whole day in frustration because they were unable to get their quiet time first thing in the morning. They really believe that the devil is going to pounce on them extra hard. Actually the Bible does not even mention quiet time. The devil is going to attack us anyway, whether we miss our quiet time or not. Let us aim for perfection, but not become a neurotic over it.

Children or Men?

The sixth balance involves conquering spiritual immaturity. There is a lot of spiritual immaturity in the Christian world and in the church. We also find a lot of spiritual immaturity in Operation Mobilisation: "This brother does it, so can I;" "he is going there, I want to go there;" or, "he has got this, so I want that." Some would call this childishness, but really it's immaturity. The truly mature Christian can say, "Others may, I cannot." "Others may, I won't." For a number of years I believed, God did not want me to have a wrist watch, but I never preached against wrist watches. Now I have a wrist watch, and it is most helpful; though for a long time I was able to be without one when many had suggested I get one.

It is amazing how easily we get the "I want bug," just because we see someone else has it, and not because we need it. Generally, if we really need a thing we can obtain it. But how often we are so immature, when we see somebody else with something, then we suddenly realize we want it also. This even goes to the absurd, whereby one person has a special snack served and we get jealous. Or we discover someone that we thought was a very dedicated disciple has an iPod which we don't have, and we decide we also should have one. This is "keeping up with the Joneses." God's way is revolutionary as demonstrated in the life of Paul. For him others could have it, but he could not; others needed it, but he did not. Don't base your spiritual life on even the most dedicated Christian you know. Base it rather on the Word of God and what the Lord Jesus reveals to you.

Realistic or Legalistic?

Finally, learn to distinguish the difference between biblical and personal conviction. It is possible to get a Bible verse for almost anything. You can defend almost anything from the Bible, but only if you are willing to take isolated Bible verses out of context.

Certain things we do in Operation Mobilisation are not biblical principles. These are principles we have accepted as those which have the least amount of problems. There will always be problems, and we must learn to discern between strong, definite and unmovable principles and principles we need to operate in a particular setting.

For example, there is nothing biblical about the time schedule for eating. It is just a matter of practicality.

The spiritually mature person can discern between what is biblical and what is unique in particular situations. There are some things that are unique to OM which cannot be forced in another situation. No doubt there may be some men, who after they have left OM shake their wives at 6:30a.m. saying, "But darling, you've got to get up for your exercises or you are not a true disciple." When she rolls over and says, "Please I want to sleep," the poor fellow won't know what to do. We need SPIRITUAL BALANCE.

Chapter 27

 Actions and Reactions

I really believe, attitude is one of the most important aspects of our walk with God. If we quickly repent of wrong attitudes and other dispositional sins, it would bring about spiritual transformation. This is, of course, connected to our actions and reactions. All through the years I have sometimes sinned and failed in this area, especially at home. I sometimes have hurt people with my quick reactions in leaders and Board meetings.

About 20 years ago two leaders gave me (maybe I requested it) good solid reasons to why not react too quickly, especially in any harsh or unkind way. Keep in mind, that in some areas a quick reaction can save a life, but we are not talking about that here. I was given two lists which I typed and pasted into my old Bible.

I was sharing these lists at a team meeting in Forest Hill (London) and my faithful secretary urged me to include these two powerful, biblical lists. So, here they are.

Ten Reasons not to overreact

1. I may be wrong!
2. It makes the other person overdefensive.
3. It is fleshy and not of the Spirit.
4. It breaks the unity.
5. It can hurt others.
6. It is not biblical.
7. It shows a wrong concept of God—forgetting that he is sovereign, in control.
8. It shows a wrong concept of man—we are made in the image of God, he/she must be handled properly.
9. It shows impatience—"Let every man be quick to hear, slow to speak, slow to anger."
10. Christ, our example, did not overreact.

Ten Reasons for not reacting to things

1. Because it often reflects our fallen personalities and not biblical principles.
2. It often *hurts people* of opposite views without helping them.
3. *It creates an emotional atmosphere* in which rational discussion and true "walking in the light" is difficult.
4. It creates a series of swings of the pendulum in counter-reactions rather than finding the right balance.
5. It makes people fearful of sharing their thoughts the next time
6. It often involves the flesh and therefore actually grieves the work of the Holy Spirit.
7. It degrades the other person as a human being because of not treating them with true value.
8. It tends to focus on the negative rather than the positive.
9. It can hurt our testimony to non-believers when they are present.
10. The scars of reaction may take years to heal, if ever.

ISBN : 978-81-7362-278-6
Pages. 148

Out Of
the comfort
Zone
by George Verwer

Authentic Media Publications. Contact: sales@ombooks.org

ISBN : 978-81-7362-164-2
Pages. 188

ISBN : 978-81-7362-146-8
Pages. 126

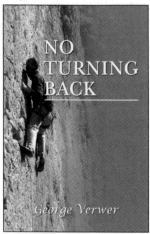

No Turning Back
by George Verwer

There Is Dynamite in Literature
by George Verwer

ISBN : 978-81-7362-627-2
Pages. 127

ISBN : 978-81-7362-152-9
Pages. 96

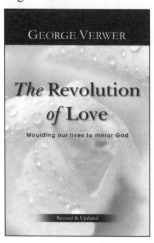

The Revolution of Love
by George Verwer

Hunger for Reality
by George Verwer

Authentic Media Publications. Contact: sales@ombooks.org

ISBN:978-0-9764290-2-9

Pages. 264

ISBN:978-81-7362-470-4

Pages. 140

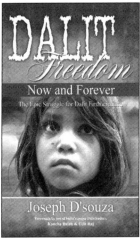

Dalit Freedom
by Joseph D'souza

Aids and You
by Dr. Patrick Dixon

ISBN:978-971-724-116-6

Pages. 122

Global
Vision . Passion . Action

by L.E. Maxwell
With Don Richardson and Paul Maxwell

ISBN:978-81-7362-872-6

Pages. 211

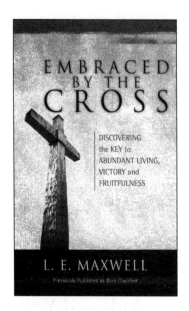

Embraced by the Cross

by L.E. Maxwell

ISBN:978-1-85078-762-4

Pages. 192

ISBN:978-81-7362-875-7

Pages. 103

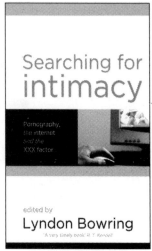

Discipleship

by Peter Maiden

Searching for intimacy

by Lyndon Bowring

Authentic Media Publications. Contact: sales@ombooks.org